Conversations with Sterling Plumpp

Literary Conversations Series
Monika Gehlawat
General Editor

Conversations
with Sterling Plumpp

Edited by John Zheng

University Press of Mississippi   Jackson

www.upress.state.ms.us

The University Press of Mississippi is a member of the Association of American University Presses.

Permission to print the following poems is granted by Sterling Plumpp.

From *Blues Narratives*: lines from Canto 5
From *Home/Bass*: "Eight," "From the Delta," "On Credit," "Gathering Place," "Rituals," lines from "My Name," lines from "Identity," and lines from "I Cry"
From *Ornate with Smoke*: lines from "Law Giver in the Wilderness"
From *Velvet BeBop Kente Cloth*: "Eight"

First printing 2016
∞
Library of Congress Cataloging-in-Publication Data

Names: Zheng, Jianqing, editor.
Title: Conversations with Sterling Plumpp / edited by John Zheng.
Description: Jackson : University Press of Mississippi, 2016. | Series:
   Literary conversations series | Includes index.
Identifiers: LCCN 2015043759 | ISBN 9781496807427 (hardback)
Subjects: LCSH: Plumpp, Sterling, 1940-—Interviews. | BISAC: LITERARY
   COLLECTIONS / American / General. | LITERARY CRITICISM / Poetry. |
   BIOGRAPHY & AUTOBIOGRAPHY / Literary.
Classification: LCC PS3566.L79 Z46 2016 | DDC 811/.54—dc23 LC record available at http://
lccn.loc.gov/2015043759

British Library Cataloging-in-Publication Data available

Books by Sterling D. Plumpp

Poetry

Portable Soul. Chicago: Third World Press, 1969. Revised edition, 1974.

Half Black Half Blacker. Chicago: Third World Press, 1970.

Muslim Men. Chicago: Broadside Press, 1972.

Steps to Break the Circle. Chicago: Third World Press, 1974.

Clinton. Detroit: Broadside Press, 1976.

The Mojo Hands Call, I Must Go. New York: Thunder's Mouth Press, 1982.

Blues: The Story Always Untold. Chicago: Another Chicago Press, 1989.

Johannesburg and Other Poems. Chicago: Another Chicago Press, 1993.

Horn Man. Chicago: Third World Press, 1995.

Ornate with Smoke. Chicago: Third World Press, 1997.

Blues Narratives. Chicago: Tia Chucha Press, 1999.

Velvet BeBop Kente Cloth. Chicago: Third World Press, 2003.

Home/Bass. Chicago: Third World Press, 2013.

Nonfiction

Black Rituals. Chicago: Third World Press, 1972; 5th rpt. Third World Press, 1991.

Edited Books

Somehow We Survive: An Anthology of South African Writing. New York: Thunder's Mouth Press, 1982.

Steel Pudding: Writing from the Gary Historical and Cultural Society Writer's Workshop. Gary, Indiana: Gary Historical and Cultural Society, 2008.

Contents

Introduction

In 2014 Sterling Plumpp, a Mississippi native and Chicago blues poet, was awarded the American Book Award for *Home/Bass*, his thirteenth and latest poetry collection. Although recognition of his status as the most original and gifted blues poet of our times has been growing, Plumpp's work is still "so very necessary and deserves far more attention than it has gotten—even with an American Book Award" (Harris).

Undoubtedly, as a poet who has been writing and publishing for five decades, Plumpp has managed to create a unique style of blues poetry that distinguishes him from other contemporary poets and reveals the profound influence of African American history, music, and vernacular. In a sense, his poetry is a call and response between him and his ancestry, between his personal tongue and the black vernacular, between his innovative blues rhythm and the blues music. Plumpp elaborates this call-and-response karma in his preface to *Ornate with Smoke*, "I perceive my ancestors invented and reinvented many languages in order to spread literacy among embattled souls: Negro Spirituals, Folktales, Sermons, Blues, Jazz, Gospel, Soul, Do-wop, and Rap. As a poet, I see these linguistic inventions as launching pads where my imagination is free to search eternity for an appropriate language for me to get through another day. I have no past, no present, and no future unless I invent language to evoke it" (x). Here he looks at his ancestry, invented language, and sensibility to African American music from a globalized angle. Although he has invented a language and mastered the forms of blues and jazz for his poetic expressivity, his territorial imagination has driven him to continue his quest, invention, and writing so that his poetry will keep pulsating with the past, present, and future. He believes that "one has to locate one's individuality and improvise nuances to suit one's personal tongue. The invented language of blues empowers the poet to speak his name and his journeying through naming pains while the invented language of jazz allows the poet to acquire a map of the territory of imaginations that changes and expands" (x).

The noted scholar Houston Baker once suggested, after surveying the limitations of the traditional critical and interpretive scheme on the Harlem

Renaissance, that "the analysis of discursive strategies" he designated as "the mastery of form" and "the deformation of mastery" produced "more accurate and culturally enriching interpretations of the *sound* and *sounding* of Afro-American modernism than do traditional methods" (xvi). To Baker, form "is not a single, easily identifiable structure" but "a symbolizing fluidity" (16–17). He postulated that the minstrel mask played an important role in these two strategies. While the mastery of form carries the tradition forward with the fluidity of sound—a deep-rooted African American voice—the deformation of mastery refuses the accepted or established form in order to obtain "the fluid and multiform mask of African ancestry" (56–57). If the form reflects tradition, the deformation reflects variations of tradition, and these variations represent new ways of expressivity while still maintaining and enriching tradition.

The dichotomy of Baker's two theoretical terms offers me a way to think associatively. Form and deformation are the twofold parts of mask. Originating from the same source, they work in terms of continuum, which reminds me of the mask changing or *bian lian* in the traditional Sichuan opera in China. In performance mask is a form of traditional, dramatic art or an image but it is not the unchangeable one. The performer must master the mask-changing skills. To present the mixed feelings of happiness, anger, sadness, grief, or surprise, he wears layers of vividly painted masks and switches magically from one mask to another in quick succession. The mask-changing skills include tearing off, rubbing, hand-waving or blowing away a mask, and a skillful performer is able to change masks eight to eighteen times. The mastery of form (mask), in response to Baker's terms, can be enriched or extended with the fluid and multiform mask of Sichuan opera.

And in literature, the mastery of form can be a strategy to produce new forms, and the form itself can be formless. The mastery requires a writer to penetrate the form to grasp the inner quality in order to deform or transform the ways of expressivity. In conformity with what the Chinese Tang-dynasty scholar Sikong Tu says in *Twenty-four Styles of Poetry*, this penetration or transformation is "to pass over the external form of image so as to attain the center of the circle" (translation is mine). In other words, this passing over for attainment is a way of transformation for the essence of what one wants to grasp. In the case of Sterling Plumpp's poetry, if blues and jazz are the fluidity of African American music, his poetry has deformed or transformed them by reimaging the music and resuscitating the language through the polyphony of voices and rhythms. His poems produced at different stages exemplify the change of form into every other form as in the ever-changing formation of wind-driven clouds. In each change or transformation, we see by ears the controlling sound of each musician, like Von Freeman in *Horn Man*, Fred Anderson in *Velvet BeBop Kente Cloth*, Willie Kent in *Home/ Bass*, and the poet himself in *Blues Narratives*. And the attainment of the changing form or the multiform presentation of the soundings indicates Plumpp's effort in maintaining and developing African American music through black vernacular. It also shows that the fluidity of form has been flowing in his blood. The presentations of these musicians' voices reveal Plumpp's effort to honor tradition and his ability to transform blues into a kind of music vibrating with his invented language. He mentions this transformation in his acknowledgments of the beboppers in *Velvet BeBop Kente Cloth*, saying, "The genius and dedication of these creators are exemplary for artists seeking to grow and know the limits of their craft in any age. Fred Anderson, in particular, continues to demonstrate that Be-Bop did not end its development when Bird passed on to ancestry. It continues each instance someone with axe in hand strives to know the parameters of his horn or piano or drum or bass and to speak that knowledge in a personal language of Bop. . . . His tenor axe taught me Be-Bop speech" (ix). Plumpp's axe, however, is his pen that chops for transformation and preserves the poetic voices through various ways of expressivity.

Blues and jazz have been the warp and woof of Plumpp's poetry. He has been writing blues and jazz poetry for five decades since his migration to Chicago, his promised land. Reading his poems, one can have a vis-à-vis encounter with a poet in a bluesman's voice that grabs you immediately. The effect of this immediacy is produced through Plumpp's mastery of form and transformation of the voices. Reginald Gibbons points out this effect in his introduction to *Home/Bass*, saying "There's a blues sound in all these poems as-if-in-the-voice-of-Willie-Kent. The poems are not blues lyrics; instead, they contain echoes and overtones of blues lyrics" (xvi). Now read these lines from *Home/Bass*:

My
business
is language, naming and
naming, using and
re-using.
You
can/purchase a quarter/of

myth/from my
tongue/for a hand
shake and/a pinch/of
loneliness. (23)

This is the voice of Willie Kent; this is also the voice of Plumpp through Kent. These lines are exemplary in that the unification of voices into one and the simplicity of words into fluidity do reflect Plumpp's mastery of the blues rhythm and the mastery of the black vernacular.

Technically speaking, the fluidity of Plumpp's poetic style is the cadence and rhythm of a southern black music and culture inherited in his coming-of-age years in Mississippi and blended into his northern urban life in Chicago. His poetry avoids the refrain of blues but he keeps its rhythm because what he intends to effect in his poetry is the blues moments through the use of blues rhythm, figurative language common to audience, and slashes. The use of slashes has been a staple in Plumpp's poetry because he believes that slashes create pauses that one can hear in a blues song. Another characteristic that distinguishes him as an original blues poet is his use of line breaks. Because he has spent fifty years watching and listening to blues singers, this invaluable experience has made his poetry read like blues. When he writes, his past experience flows out with a spontaneous fluidity of form he has mastered.

Even though he has staunchly written blues poetry, used the black vernacular to vivify and sophisticate the ways of creative expression, and been acclaimed as "the finest blues poet . . . standing next to Hughes" (Ward) and one of the most original American poets (Gibbons), Plumpp has not yet received enough critical attention. This situation exists probably owing to that his mastery of blues expressivity and blues deformation has seldom pleased the mainstream, but he seems not to care much about not being in the spotlight. He knows from the bottom of his heart that his task is to write about his people, his culture, and his ancestry; as he states in the MPB interview by Diane Williams, "part of my task in life is to use language to speak about the humanity of African Americans to affirm that humanity and to be proud of the legacy of the people who developed Negro spirituals, blues, jazz, and gospel." This indomitable spirit has raised Plumpp's awareness to perceive, to feel, and to be conscious of African Americans and to invent the language to present their feelings through his ceaseless exploration of the blues expressivity. With this unyielding spirit, Plumpp has never sought for his poetry any other modes of expression or poetic structures such as sonnet or other traditional forms. His poetry is an embodiment of Chicago blues, a blend of the country blues and Rock 'n' Roll.

Moreover, Plumpp's use of black vernacular for his blues expressivity is as simplistic and sophisticated as Muddy Waters's use of slide guitar for an effect similar to jazz, because Plumpp is the finest blues lyricist who has been mainly influenced by Muddy Waters's engagement of vernacular. Plumpp says in his interview conducted by John Zheng on March 18, 2015, "A writer has choices to make in terms of the voice of the persona. . . . I'm writing poetry, and there is something about both the tone and the phrasing of Muddy Waters that forces me to try and create a line that suggests blues, or to create a line that suggests blues even while a persona is engaged in ordinary dialogue." Fortunately, his simplicity and sophistication in the use of language has been recognized by the trustworthy critic Theodore Haddin, who writes that Plumpp has "come a long way in his love of non-standard English (I won't just call it vernacular), the language spoken and sung by jazz musicians whose language goes back to the root of soul-word deeds, the unhassled, unhampered freedom of utterance that combines song into poem. If we don't understand at first what he means, we can study his words till we do. They cause us to wrestle back into the way words first came into existence in English and reveal that root of speech that reduces terms to uninhibited expression." That "they cause us to wrestle" surely produces an effect of territorial transformation of the black vernacular and challenges us to consider what is behind the words or sounds of Plumpp's blues poetry and what is behind the dynamics of his bondage to African American culture.

Plumpp is an important American poet of the twentieth and the twenty-first centuries. His root has grown deep and spread wide in both the southern rural and the northern urban land, moistened by the rich history of African American culture, music, and vernacular. His unique style reflects his territorial imagination through the guitar striking blues and the horn blowing jazz. He deserves a more extensive reading. As the scholar Jerry Ward asserts, "At the crossroads of blues and jazz, reading Plumpp's poetry is an act of metamorphosis." There is no doubt that reading Plumpp is like searching for the mask or form of expression. In this reading process, one gains joy through the rhythmic sounds heard by eyes, thus raising awareness of the importance of language, specifically the African American vernacular.

In almost fifty years, Plumpp has published thirteen poetry books, one book about black psychology, and two edited anthologies. The American

Book Award he received in 2014 has given him a leap forward to writing, and currently his focus has shifted from the promised land of Chicago to the native soil of Mississippi where he serves as a writer-in-residence at Mississippi Valley State University. In the birthplace of the Delta blues, Plumpp has found new subjects to write. Touring in the Delta to visit blues sites, he has been amazed by the fact of how the blues luminaries had achieved vernacular eloquence in a place where they remained completely anonymous as farmhands, and his plan is, in his own words, to "write about the place as being the humus out of which African Americans farm the culture, out of which I try to create my art" (Zheng, "Muddy Waters").

This collection includes fourteen interviews with and on Sterling Plumpp, most of which have been published in literary magazines and scholarly journals or aired on the radio. Within these interviews, Plumpp addresses numerous inquiries about his growing up in rural Mississippi; his high school and college education; his parents and grandparents; his reading and writing about blues and jazz; his travels to South Africa and Australia; his distant association with the Black Arts Movement and the Organization of Black American Culture; his comments on Afrocentrism, decolonization, church, racism and slavery; his visions of black aesthetic, black arts legacy, and black power; and, most importantly, his friendship and connection with blues and jazz musicians and his development and innovation as a poet. These interviews reveal numerous aspects of his life. For instance, his childhood continues to provide him with rich sources for writing, as witnessed in his talk about his mother—a dominant figure in his poetry book *Blues Narratives*—in the interview from Reginald Gibbons:

> She *is* the reason that I'm here. And there's nothing I can do about my childhood, the first sixteen or seventeen years of my life. She was not blessed with longevity so I could sit and talk to her about this complex kind of relationship I suppose she and I had. But I also knew that I couldn't go forward without dealing with that part of the puzzle of my existence. I tried to deal with it when she died in 1980. And I couldn't. And it's only somewhere between 1995 and 2000 that I developed a kind of formula of how I could deal with the fact that I had been born a peasant and somehow been educated, and she had been born a peasant and her imagination seemed to remain within the orbit of folk dictates.

Changing from a college student to a post office clerk and then to a poet, critic, editor and professor since the late 1960s, Plumpp has been asked about the writers and musicians who have influenced him. He easily identifies three African American luminaries. He speaks in a humorous tone that the words of Richard Wright excite an unquenchable hunger; he talks about Amiri Baraka's poetic style that renders blues into bebop and uses ellipsis to achieve quick phrasing and his ability to integrate all kinds of art elements into a poem; and he draws a vivid sketch of Louis Armstrong who played two instruments—trumpet and voice—and who played his voice better than he played the trumpet. To Michael Antonucchi, Plumpp states that one will not know much about African American culture if one does not look at it through blues and the African American church. Equally frequent with interviewers are questions about his writing and creative development. He says in the following interview from Jerry Ward:

> I knew I wanted to write. I knew I wanted to create a particular vision of the world that my past had given me a vantage to see. I wrote fragments of poems. I listened to music a great deal. At some point, all of this synthesized and I tried to write poetry. Much of that poetry culminated in my attempt to be elliptical in my expression, to be sparse with quick rhythm and quick imagery. Not imagery of the absurd but imagery of the black experience. A great deal of that resulted in *Portable Soul*. Also, trying to give multiple meaning to words by the way they are placed on paper, so that linguistic as well as rhythmic experiences occur. But my own feeling is that *Portable Soul* is philosophical. At that point I had begun to play the black base.

The above narration reveals a fact that although *Portable Soul* is his first poetry book published by Third World Press in 1969, Plumpp had already realized by then the significance of African American music and its influence on his writing, the imagery of black experience, the rhythm of expression, and the effort in giving meaning beyond meaning to words. Over the years his style—a confluence of southern and urban black music sounding with the impulse of black vernacular and experience—has remained strong and become an inseparable part of black aesthetic. But to say Plumpp is just a blues poet limits one's vision to understanding his poetry. He belongs to the world. By telling his stories, Plumpp tells the stories of African American people; by telling the stories of African American people, he tells the stories this world should know. Therefore, Plumpp is a poet in a global sense.

The interviews are arranged in chronological order according to the dates they were conducted. Given that they cover a span of thirty-five years, there is repetition of some subject matter such as Plumpp's background and education, but each interview presents a different profile of Plumpp at a different time. Graham Hodges's interview touches on Plumpp's stint as a political activist in the 1960s and the connection between his poetry and jazz; Jerry Ward's long, atypical but original "collage interview" offers an exploratory examination of how Plumpp sensed the world and why he depicted the vision as he did as an artist in the early 1980s; half of Toni Costonie's interview recounts Plumpp's travel to Australia; the one conducted by Michael Antonucchi presents Plumpp's idea about black church, OBAC, and Black Arts; his experience as a writer and editor in the 1960s and 1970s; his travel to South Africa; and his clarification that he "was not a Black Arts poet poured from some mold" but one who attempts to create a poet for himself. Reginald Gibbons's lengthy interview, which took him seven years to transcribe, provides details about Plumpp's family, education, life, and political involvement in Chicago; about his comments on Gwendolyn Brooks, James Baldwin, Don L. Lee, African American history, and imagination; and about his teaching and writing. While Dike Okoro's interview goes over Plumpp's vision as a poet with a discussion of *Velvet BeBop Kente Cloth*, John Edgar Wideman's conversation gives an eloquent account of Plumpp as a friend and an artist in the truest sense. Hermine Pinson's short phone interview questions Plumpp on musical genres other than blues and jazz that inform his poetry and how his migration to the Midwest affected his perspective; James Ballowe's interview presents a fresh perspective on Plumpp's status as the poet of the ear, and the three interviews conducted by me have three different focal points: the first one is on Plumpp's bluesjazz poetry and discussion of a few poems selected for the interview, and the other two are respectively on his award-winning book *Home/Bass* and on the influence of Muddy Waters. Mamie Osborne's interview centers on Plumpp's experience as the writer-in-residence at Mississippi Valley State University; and the last interview, conducted by Diane Williams for the Mississippi Public Broadcasting, focuses on the poet's return to Mississippi and his career as a writer.

I had the idea of editing this conversations book back in 2013 after I received my second grant from the National Endowment for the Humanities to conduct summer workshops on three African American writers including Sterling Plumpp. He came down from Chicago by train to participate in the two-day workshop on his poetry. During his stay, we had several good chats over southern food, on the country road to Money and blues sites, and in the waiting room of the Greenwood Amtrak Station. I also need to mention that since we first met in 2005 at the panel on his poetry at

Arkansas State University, I have had the privilege to run a special issue on him in *Valley Voices: A Literary Review* and invite him to do a poetry reading on our campus. I believe that the publication of this book will be of great significance to African American literature and of special interest to both academics and common readers since Plumpp's poetry comes from the language used in daily life.

My sincere thanks go to the interviewers and the copyright holders who generously granted me permission to include their work and to a number of people who have helped me with this project: my editor Katie Keene for working with me on the book and for her patience with me to finish the project, Craig Gill for reviewing the manuscript, other UPM staff such as Anne Stascavage and Shane Gong Stewart for their help behind the scenes, Philip Kolin and Jerry Ward for their valuable suggestions, Diane Ross for sending me a copy of the *Southern Quarterly* containing Jerry Ward's interview I needed urgently, Gwendolyn Mitchell for typing three interviews, Samuel Melton for scanning two interviews, Seprela Ellis for transcribing two interviews, Deb Purnell for scanning the Toni Costonie interview from the University of Mississippi Library, Jo Baldwin for reading the introduction, and, of course, Sterling D. Plumpp.

JZ

Works Cited

Baker, Houston. *Modernism and the Harlem Renaissance.* Chicago: U of Chicago P, 1987.

Gibbons, Reginald. Introduction. *Home/Bass.* Chicago: Third World P, 2013. xiii–xviii.

Haddin, Theodore. "Message to the author." March 4, 2015. E-mail.

Harris, Duriel E. "Permission for using Sterling Plumpp's Interview." Message to the author. March 27, 2015. E-mail.

Plumpp, Sterling. Acknowledgments. *Velvet BeBop Kente Cloth.* Chicago: Third World P, 2003.

———. *Home/Bass.* Chicago: Third World P, 2013.

———. Preface. *Ornate with Smoke.* Chicago: Third World P, 1997. ix–x.

Sikong, Tu. *Twenty-four Styles of Poetry.* http://web.it.nctu.edu.tw/~lccpan/newpage411.htm.

Ward, Jerry. "Reading Sterling D. Plumpp." http://projecthbw.blogspot.com/2013/01/reading-sterling-d-plumpp.html.

Zheng, John. "Muddy Waters: A Conversation with Sterling D. Plumpp." *Arkansas Review* 46.3 (2015) March 18, 2015.

Chronology

1940	Born Sterling Dominic Plumpp on January 30 on a plantation in Clinton, Mississippi, to Cyrus H. Plumpp and Mary Emmanuel. Reared by maternal grandparents Victor and Mattie Emmanuel, who are sharecroppers.
1948	Attends a grammar school ten miles away.
1955	Grandfather dies. Moves to Jackson, Mississippi, and attends Holy Ghost High School there.
1956	Converts to Catholicism.
1960	Graduates as valedictorian from high school.
1960–62	Wins scholarship to attend Saint Benedict's College in Atchison, Kansas. One of the seven black students on campus; given a job to sweep the Administrative Building and the dormitory.
1961	Goes to Chicago to look for a summer job.
1962	Quits college and goes to Chicago.
1962–64	Works as a distribution clerk in the Chicago Main Post Office.
1964–65	Serves in the army for two years.
1965	Father dies.
1966–69	Works as a distribution clerk in the Chicago Main Post Office.
1968	Earns BA in psychology from Roosevelt University in Chicago. Publishes first poem "Black Hands" in the September issue of *Negro Digest.*
1969	*Portable Soul* is published by Third World Press. Becomes a member of OBAC (Organization of Black American Culture).
1969–71	Works as a counselor at North Park College in Chicago.
1970	*Half Black Half Blacker* is published by Third World Press.
1970–73	Assistant editor for Third World Press.
1070–76	Book reviewer for *Negro Digest/Black World.*
1971	Completes all graduate courses in psychology from Roosevelt University.
1971–72	Lecturer in the Black Studies Program at the University of Illinois at Chicago.

1971–73	Serves as director of Institute of Positive Education and as managing editor, *Black Books Bulletin.*
1972	*Muslim Men* is published by Broadside Press. Leaves OBAC. *Black Rituals*, a collection of essays, is published by Third World Press.
1972–76	Instructor in the Black Studies Program at the University of Illinois at Chicago.
1973	Poetry in *The Poetry of Black America* (Harper and Row).
1974	*Steps to Break the Circle* is published by Third World Press.
1975	Wins the Illinois Arts Council Literary Award for "Clinton" published in *Savage.* Receives Third World Press Tenth Anniversary Builder's Award.
1976	*Clinton* is published by Broadside Press. Receives the First Broadside Press Publisher's Award and the Silver Circle Award for Excellence in Teaching.
1977	Poetry in *Griefs of Joy: Anthology of Contemporary Afro-American Poetry for Students* (Black River Writers).
1977–84	Assistant professor in the Black Studies Program at the University of Illinois at Chicago.
1979	Wins the Illinois Arts Council Literary Award for "Fractured Dreams" published in *Another Chicago Magazine.*
1980	Mother dies. Wins the Illinois Arts Council Literary Award for "The Mojo Hands Call, I Must Go" published in *Another Chicago Magazine.*
1981–82	Has encounter with Von Freeman.
1982	*The Mojo Hands Call, I Must Go*, a collection of autobiographical poems, and *Somehow We Survive: An Anthology of South African Writing* are published by Thunder's Mouth Press. Serves as poetry editor of *Black American Literature Forum.* The Sterling D. Plumpp Collection is archived at the University of Mississippi Library.
1983	Wins the Carl Sandburg Literary Prize for Poetry for the poetry collection *The Mojo Hands Call, I Must Go* and the Creative Writing Award for Excellence in Poetry from DuSable Museum of African American History.
1984	Serves as poet-in-residence, Evanston School, Illinois, and Youth Black Heritage Theater Ensemble Studio. Works as director of Young Writer's Workshop for Urban Gateways. *Warbell*, a four-act play, is written.

1984–94   Associate professor in the Black Studies Program at the University of Illinois at Chicago.

1985   *Mojo Hands, A Blues Drama* is written and adapted for the stage by Virginia Boyle. Appears in *Dictionary of Literary Biography*, Volume XLI: *Afro-American Poets Since 1955*, Gale. Reads at the Old State Capitol Museum (Mississippi State Historical Museum) during the 1985 Mississippi Writer's Day. "Mighty Long River" (short story) appears in *Mississippi Writers: Reflections of Childhood of Youth*, published by University Press of Mississippi.

1986   *STREETS, A One Act Poem* is written and presented at the jazz and blues event Night Mojo.

1988   Poetry is included in *Mississippi Writers: Reflections of Childhood and Youth* (University Press of Mississippi). Invited guest writer of the state in New South Wales, Australia.

1989   *Blues: The Story Always Untold* is published by Another Chicago Press.

1991   Commissioned by the Swiss Consulate to write the libretto "My Feeling Tone" for Swiss composer George Gruntz's *Chicago Cantana* which has its world premiere performance at the Chicago Jazz Festival in August and performance in Switzerland and China. Presentation at the International Writers Symposium in Johannesburg, South Africa. Visits South Africa.

1992   Poetry is included in *Black Southern Voices: An Anthology* (Meridian Book) and *Men of Our Time: An Anthology of Male Poetry in Contemporary America* (University of Georgia Press).

1993   *Johannesburg and Other Poems* is published by Another Chicago Press. Grandmother Mattie dies.

1994–2002 Professor in the Black Studies Program and English at the University of Illinois at Chicago.

1995   *Horn Man*, a collection of poems dedicated to legendary Chicago tenor saxophonist Von Freeman, is published by Third World Press. Serves as an advisor for the television production of the documentary *The Promised Land*. A poem in *Mississippi Observed* (University Press of Mississippi). Visits South Africa as an invited guest of the African National Congress of South Africa.

1996   Poetry is included in *The Best American Poetry 1996, The Garden Thrives: Twentieth-Century African-American Poetry* (Harper

	Perennial), and *Trouble the Water: 250 Years of African American Poetry* (Signet).
1997	*Ornate with Smoke* is published by Third World Press. Biography is included in *The Oxford Companion to African-American Literature.*
1999	*Blues Narratives* is published by Tia Chucha Press. Receives the Richard Wright Literary Excellence Award from the Natchez Literary and Cinema Celebration.
2000	Inducted into the International Literary Hall of Fame for Writers of African Descent, Chicago State University.
2001	Wins $1 million in the Illinois Lottery. Receives special recognition with a symposium hosted by the University of Illinois at Chicago to celebrate the distinguished career of Sterling Plumpp.
2002	Retires as professor emeritus of English and African American studies. Invited poet at Jazz Festival in Toulouse, France.
2002–12	Visiting professor of English at Chicago State University.
2003	*Velvet BeBop Kente Cloth* is published by Third World Press.
2004	Poetry is included in *African American Literature* (Penguin Academics) and *Furious Flower* (University of Virginia Press). Receives the Keeping the Blues Alive Award from the Blues Foundation.
2005	A special panel on Sterling Plumpp is held at the Delta Blues Symposium XI, Arkansas State University, in April. A special section of the December issue of *Arkansas Review: A Journal of Delta Studies* is devoted to Sterling Plumpp. Receives the River Road Lifetime Achievement Award from the Mississippi Valley Blues Society.
2006	Poetry is included in *The Oxford Anthology of African American Literature.*
2007	Invited guest of the James and Marilou Kelly Writers Series on November 4. Biography is included in *Encyclopedia of African American Literature.*
2008	*Steel Pudding: Writing from the Gary Historical and Cultural Society Writer's Workshop* is published.
2009	A special issue of *Valley Voices: A Literary Review* is devoted to criticism on Sterling Plumpp's poetry.
2010	Invited poet of the Lyceum Lecture Series at Mississippi Valley State University, accompanied by jazz saxophonist Kenny Blake from Pittsburgh.

2011   Biography is included in *The Cambridge History of African American Literature.*

2013   *Home/Bass*, a poetry book celebrating the Mississippi-born, Chicago bass player Willie Kent, is published by Third World Press. Receives a tribute from the Guild Literary Complex (May 14). Funded by a grant from the National Endowment for the Humanities, the 2013 NEH Summer Workshops at Mississippi Valley State University, with a theme of "African American Literary Heritage: Three Mississippi Writers," devotes a two-day session, led by Hermine Pinson, to the discussion and exploration of Plumpp's poetry and aesthetics. His reading is accompanied by jazz saxophonist Alphonso Sanders.

2014   Receives the American Book Award for *Home/Bass*; wins the Illinois Arts Council Agency Literary Award for "Mississippi Suite" published in *TriQuarterly*. A special feature of eight poems and an interview on *Home/Bass* in *Poetry South*.

2015   Receives the Lifetime Achievement Award from the University of Illinois at Chicago; serves as writer-in-residence at Mississippi Valley State University; conducts three delta blues tours, guided by John Zheng. Poetry reading at MVSU, accompanied by jazz saxophonist Alphonso Sanders and percussionist Ben Arnold.

Conversations with Sterling Plumpp

Amiri Baraka, Sterling Plumpp, and Curtis Lyle: An Interview

Graham Hodges / 1982

From *Another Chicago Magazine* 12 (1985): 186–94. Reprinted by permission of *Another Chicago Magazine*.

The following interview occurred as a part of the Conversations with Writers Series at the New School for Social Research in New York City during March 1982, the interview was part of a special presentation of jazz and poetry. Before the interview, Amiri Baraka, Sterling Plumpp, and K. Curtis Lyle, accompanied by alto saxophonist Julius Hemphill, regaled a capacity crowd with two hours of readings. The reading was produced and moderated by Graham Hodges who also conducted the interview.

GH: I wish to introduce the general theme of the evening about the connections between jazz and poetry by asking Sterling Plumpp when he first became aware of the potentials of these connections.

SP: Two points about my life. One is that I always wanted to be a blues singer and somehow got indicated out of the singing of blues or did not have the work. But actually I had an unusual career in that at the time I began reading, the writers I read—particularly Amiri Baraka—were people who were jazz influenced. I read his works. I was trying to write rhymed poems. And the rhyme was not working and I was trying to control the lines. So listening to music and going to see music added meaning to my theme. Music made me discover that I was southern; I watch the blues in person at least five hours a week.

GH: Where do you do this now?

SP: In Chicago. Two of the better blues musicians are Little Bill Harrington on lead guitar who can do everything that Jimi Hendrix could and more and he's only about twenty-three. I believe the *New York Times* said he's the greatest guitarist in the world. And there's a young brother on harmonica named Billy Branch who does Little Walter and Sonny Boy Williamson's (Rice Miller's) tradition a great deal of justice.

GH: Curtis Lyle, you're from Los Angeles and there is a very strong idiom of blues music in Los Angeles and I wonder if that had been one of the influences on your poetry and on your accent on jazz.

CL: I think that my fascination with the music comes from my childhood. My father was a bass player. Two of my uncles were musicians also. So the first music that I heard in my house was Lester Young and Billy Holiday. I was six or seven years old. I didn't know what it really was, but it was the first thing I ever heard. My connection with the blues basically comes from soldiering in St. Louis. I lived in St. Louis for five years from '69 to '74. St. Louis has quite a reputation as an old blues city. It's not quite as functional as it once was, but when I got to St. Louis I discovered basically the Delta blues: Blind Lemon Jefferson, East Texas, and Skip James, Mississippi Delta. Blind Lemon was from Texas, but in the Delta I found Son House. The holy blues actually I think has had a greater influence on my work, being a kind of religious blues singing coming out of maybe somebody like Gary Davis or Blind Willie Johnson. So these are basically my connections to the music. So, in Los Angeles the particular group that I came out of in terms of poetry is called the Watts Writers' Workshop. Most of the people in the workshop were expelled collegians, people who have been turned off by college. So when we came together there were people who had been raised in the church. There was the budding Rasta movement on the west coast at that time also. So all these forces came together in our poetry, and of course, not trying to embarrass him but probably the greatest influence I think on us literally was Baraka. So like Sterling said, *The Dead Lecturer*, perhaps *Twenty Volume Suicide Note*, things like this, this is what lead us into what we have recently done with poetry.

GH: Okay, with that we should turn to Mr. Baraka as the author of those influential works and find out who his mentors were and what led him into this association of jazz and poetry.

AB: In the black community music is always the freest thing around. Everything has a string on it tied up to White racist monopoly capitalism. Even the music. But the music seems freest, and I think that's why we gravitate to it. And poetry actually is a form of music anyway, I think. A lot of times we don't know that because we read academic American poetry; we think it's a form of dullness. But really poetry is a form of music. Most of the poetry that's written by the academy is not intended to be read at all. It's usually meant so people can get tenure in universities and then it goes to a library. But I think that for those of us who are interested in people hearing it and listening to it, it always has to be close to music, 'cause that's where it began. That's where poetry began; close to music, close to dance, and for those of us who are in the Afro-American community it's normal that that music should be the music of our own people because that's what we come up with. That's what we're born with, so that's music. So unless you've been actually lobotomized by the university where you've been taught to think that something else is hipper than what you know is hip, then the music that you grew up with would be normally the music that you would use to make your strongest statements. And we grew up with the city blues. The Quartets, Dinah Washington, Ruth Brown, the Ravens, that was my teenage life. Larry Darnell was the first poet that I ever heard because Larry Darnell, between singing the blues, would come out and he would recite. And we used to, all of us when we were teenagers, we used to learn that poetry had great, great style to it. The first poetry that I knew was the poetry of the blues. That's the first poetry that had any meaning to me.

GH: So then blues and jazz permit you, or assist you, in getting closer to a people's form of poetry?

AB: I think that there are so many constraints and limitations to getting to your actual consciousness as a free being, aside from what America has put on you, especially for an oppressed people. They have a kind of pathology, I mean the oppressors have a pathology, the oppressed have a pathology. But in order to get through that and get to your actual free-functioning self, the music helps lead you there because the music is freer than any of the other expressions. A lot of the artists even begin to try to imitate the oppressors. They don't want to kill the oppressors. They want to beat them. But the musicians usually are freer, I mean the music is freer. Music leads you to a freer place in yourself. That makes you in tune with the people 'cause the people are in tune with the music. Blues is the popular music of Afro-American people, one kind of blues or another. So if you're in that idiom you're definitely closer to the people than what passes for culture at Lincoln Center.

GH: Do you find that it works out that way, that as you mix blues and jazz with poetry it makes your work more meaningful to people at large?

AB: Yes, absolutely, sure. When I teach writing I always tell my students, not if you think your stuff is tough, what you should do is go outside and when you see those workers after they're working on those houses, building those houses and digging in the streets and they're sitting around in the afternoon eating lunch, you should read a poem to them and see if you keep their interests or see if they try to stone you.

GH: We were talking about the relationship between poets and popular musicians. The most popular poet in this country will never sell as much as Michael Jackson. How can the connection between jazz and poetry gain a larger audience? Curtis Lyle, what do you think about that?

CL: That has not been one of my main interests. Of all the particular approaches the one that I love most is the musical. When I incorporate music into my work it makes the work larger, freer, it makes it more powerful, it connects it with a tradition that is sacred and has never been broken. Those are my interests when I connect my poetry with music. I consider myself a musician in that sense. In L.A., we used to call ourselves "word musicians." But I haven't thought of it in terms of a larger audience.

GH: That's a nice title.

CL: But that's what we were. We were word musicians and we will always be that. That's what we love and that's what we are.

GH: I noticed you have a very strong voice. Were you a singer at one time?

CL: No, I've never been a singer, but I learned from a friend of mine, a member of the Watts Writers' Workshop, who was raised in a Baptist church. And the first time I heard him read a poem—he has a poem and it's called, "Something from Mt. Oruro" or something like that, and in this poem he has a line where he says, "I have seen coal line hustlers chase asthmatic king fishes down main street over avenues of blues, floor sheen shoes, niggers paying dues and James Brown standing in the corner screaming, please, please, please. I saw the sun die, I heard the night weeping." When I heard him say that, I said goddamn. I didn't know you could do it like that because I had never had anybody show it to me like that. And once I heard that, and once everybody else in our particular workshop heard it, we sort of improvised off that and everybody got their own voice. But I think in a way he was the initiator of the particular style that came out of our place.

GH: I have more questions, but I don't want to monopolize. Are there any questions from the audience?

Audience: If it's conceded that there is a great relationship between jazz and poetry writing, Baraka, does that influence you into choosing your themes to rhyme with your poems?

AB: Well, to a certain extent. I have poems to Trane and Monk and Duke Ellington. I wrote a poem that tried to talk about all the musicians in the whole tradition that influenced me, influenced most people. Yes, it does influence, and it should because the musicians have been great upholders of the traditions of the Afro-American people. And so it's only natural that they would influence not only your form but your content. And many times I think when you write a poem it's the rhythm that starts you in motion first, even before you even know what the words are. The rhythm is the thing that makes you and then you try to get the words to match that rhythm. I could go on a long time, but yes is the answer to your question.

Aud: Sterling Plumpp, would you also respond to that question?

SP: There's two things taking place with me as a poet. I began as a political activist. I was more of an activist in the '60s than I was a poet, marching and demonstrating and other things. But I actually believe that the poetry could be made more national in terms of black culture if music and speech were incorporated creatively. That requires a great deal of work and a great deal of skill. It's not very easy to write an oral poem that is both written well and has the necessary message in it.

Aud: Baraka?

AB: One thing to add to that. Music's so powerful you can—even those of us who think that we're intelligent—you can be walking down the street and humming some song. You don't even know what the lyrics are and you'll be humming, and if somebody were to stop you and say, "What is that you're humming?" and you say, "I am a fool, I should take dope and kill myself," because those are the lyrics coming out of the top twenty, and we're all walking down the street singing—it shows you how powerful music is. Because the music that most of us sing is absolute stupidity. If you analyze the lyrics of the top twenty, somebody can get a platinum record and all they're singing is, "I want you baby, I want you baby, I want you baby, I want you baby, I want you baby, I want you baby," and it's the music that actually is making that interesting. You understand what I'm saying. But other than that, if you analyze it from the lyrics it has absolutely no value at all.

Aud: I wish to ask, particularly because Sterling Plumpp and Amiri Baraka have spent so much time in politics, how they perform the very difficult feat of mixing politics, poetry, and music?

SP: I learned two things about politics. I learned first of all you have to acknowledge self-ignorance. I had to tell myself sometime in the '60s that Sterling Plumpp was ignorant of politics. You don't understand anything about revolution. Things were happening so fast and I was very active. I couldn't make sense out of it. And so I had to do a great deal of reading. I have always been very close to people who were Marxists, and one of the great advantages is, they will tell you to shut up when they think you don't know what you're talking about. It was very educational for me in some respects because some of the times I found that they were correct when it came to politics. And I was very close to three South African poets, and some of the things that they told me about their lives left indelible marks. Dennis Brutus, Kgositsile, and Serote. I was very close to them as people. They told me about their lives, and when I read their poetry I saw how they transformed it. The official line in South Africa is that if you teach religion you have to teach the black child to say boss Jesus. That's true. It's a fact. Boss Jesus. And if you say Our Lord, it's against the state. And fortunately for me there's a very strong Afro-American tradition of writing poetry, from very gifted writers. The best poem you write could be beaten by somebody in that tradition. So you should study it. There's a great deal of talent. So that led me to the fact that I thought that I was always an apprentice. And that I might apprentice my way out of that by what I produced. That's my approach to it personally.

Aud: Baraka?

AB: People make a great deal about it if you write about politics, but everybody writes about politics. There's no such thing as apolitical poetry artists. They are people who take that stance, but even that is political. That stance supports the status quo. And like Sterling says, in terms of the Afro-American tradition, like if you read about David Walker. David Walker wrote a book called *The Appeal*. Six months later they killed him. They banned the book. If you were caught with the book you could be hanged or locked up. I'd say that's what I aspire to. I want to write a book and make them ban it. I want to make them lock people up if they have it. I want to write a poem so heavy that they have to put your picture in the post office and say, "This dude wrote this poem, lock his ass up." That's because the tradition of Afro-American writers, slave writers, writers writing against national oppression, segregation and discrimination, that's our tradition. Now somebody else might have another tradition that they aspire to. But I'll tell you this, if you study the great writers in history. Great writers? I know that the academies are going to say this and that about them. Like they're going to push Henry James, Herman Melville, and Mark Twain. You understand. They're always going to push the reactionaries. But you'll find out that there is a tradition of writers who understand the world, understand what's happening in the world, and those writers use that poetry to fight on the side of the people. And that's the tradition that I want to be in. Now people can say, that ain't art, that's social protest, that's this and that, they can give me a C in their writing class, but what I say is ultimately they will not judge it. That's my line. See, they will not be the judge of it. The people who have judged it will be the people who will know that this society needs to be destroyed. So I'm writing to them. That's what I feel about it.

GH: Given that all three of you do teach, what is the future? Do you see younger people writing or singing jazz poetry? Sterling?
SP: An interesting thing is happening because of the phonograph. In my class there are several brilliant oral poets. They can sing it, but they cannot invent the words and control them on paper. They are very interested in reading. They read all of the books of Alice Walker, or the books of Ntozake Shange. What I tell them is this: If you're oppressed when you're born, you're oppressed when you die if you don't get free. And you don't get free—the only way you get free is to take freedom. There are tremendous budgetary decisions being made that are wiping out a large number of the working class students from so-called universities ($15,000 or $20,000) that many of the sons and daughters of the middle class, who want to become engineers or doctors or lawyers, is to take the place of the working class students at state supported universities. You get people coming to universities who are literate and they want to become illiterate to become an accountant. On the one hand I'm encouraged by those people who come directly from the ghetto who are still in the university and then I'm discouraged by the reactionary tendencies in the black bourgeoisie. There are some very good writers, but there's a struggle to keep them in the universities.

GH: I was at a reading last Friday and during the evening I heard the moderator talk about rap music as mindless. I wondered if you felt that way too, or if you felt this is some form of urban poetry? Curtis?
CL: I don't think that rap music, rap poetry, is mindless. Some of it I'm not

particularly in tune to, but some of it is very profound. One of the problems, and this is back to the point that Sterling was making before, I found, and I've been teaching in universities for fourteen or fifteen years, one problem I came up against was that very bright students didn't know the extent of what poetry can be. So I would have to bring Taj Mahal records and Charlie Parker's music into the class. I found myself having to convince the students that poetry lives everywhere. Baraka said earlier that most of the lyrics to the songs that we find ourselves humming are mindless. But now and then I come across something, like one day I remember listening to a Bill Withers song. He had this one line in the song which completely blew me away. I said, that's what I want my poetry to be. He said very simply, "You either got two choices. You can lay down and be weak or you can stand up where you're at and still be strong." So I want them to know that poetry lives everywhere around them. I want them to be able to recognize poetry. One of the problems we had, especially coming out of the '60s, was that everything that comes off the street is not poetry. But then a lot of things that do come off the street are poetry. So I had to try to show them how to discriminate. I know that I completely disagree with that statement that rap music is mindless. I love Grandmaster Flash's song. It's very similar to writing poetry: "Don't push me 'cause I'm close to the edge. I'm trying not to lose my head." That's poetry to me. I want personally. I would like my poetry to be that strong and direct. I can't think of anything more directly descriptive of our lives.

GH: Amiri, you want to add anything to that?
AB: I think you ought to look at rap records like you look at everything: dialectically. You have to split them in half. There's a positive aspect and a negative aspect. Obviously the commercial forces always would like to push the mindless stuff. But despite that, the fact that it is coming from the masses themselves, coming from the roots of black culture, then some of it has to be profound because it's speaking about the people's lives. So in looking at that you have to look at it like everything else. You have to look at it dialectically; that is, you have to cut it in half. Separate that which is positive from that which is negative. The same thing with rap music. Most of what they push on the radio, TV, they're going to push the stuff that's mindless. That's what they want to push. But at the same time you're going to get Grandmaster Flash. You cannot help it because it's coming right from the roots of the people. So it's got to speak to those people if it's going to hold them.

Sterling D. Plumpp: A Son of the Blues

Jerry W. Ward, Jr. / 1984

From the *Southern Quarterly* 29.3 (Spring 1991): 5–36. Reprinted by permission of the *Southern Quarterly*.

July 1990: From the vantage of my 1984 interview with Sterling Dominic Plumpp, much has changed and much remains constant. Both change and continuity are located in Plumpp's involvement with the blues as form, history, and psychological beat. His most recent book of poetry, *Blues: The Story Always Untold* (1989), demonstrates his expanded consciousness of blues as cultural expression and his mastery of a language which the poet Raymond R. Patterson has described as "brilliantly improvisational, dazzling in technique, and thoroughly grounded in tradition."[1] Plumpp has discovered a solution in his writing to a problem hinted at in the interview: how to be a southern writer without purveying stereotypes. He talks ancestry in a global sense and resuscitates language. The growing recognition of his status as the most gifted blues poet of his generation is evidenced by Jacques Lacava's recent profile of him in *Living Blues* (March–April 1990) and the publication of his poem "Blues/scapes" in the same issue. It is not unusual now to find Plumpp's work in such music publications as *Jam Sessions* and *The Original Chicago Blues Annual*, or in *People's Tribune*, a community newspaper in Chicago. His work has begun to influence audiences having no special interest in literature.

Since 1984, Plumpp has written *Warbell*, a four-act play that deals with the consequences of migration from Mississippi to Chicago and uses the structural poetics of the blues. In 1985, he wrote *Mojo Hands, A Blues Drama*, which was adapted for the stage by Virginia Boyle; the following year, he and Boyle collaborated in presenting the jazz and blues event Night Mojo, which included Plumpp's STREETS, A One Act Poem. His experiments in writing drama wherein music is an integral feature have complemented his work on the novel-in-progress, *Mighty Long Time*, as has his writing music criticism for such publications as *Chicago Musicale.*

Poet, fiction writer, playwright, and essayist, Plumpp is a Mississippi native whose notable achievement is innovative use of the deep structures of the blues. His writing is informed, compelling and purposeful; it evokes a careful reconsideration of what can be done with literature and music as southern cultural expressions. This "collage interview" is a preliminary examination of how the man senses the world and why Plumpp as artist depicts his vision as he does. The interview was taped at Tougaloo College on 17 March 1984. Other material used comes from correspondence, Plumpp's "Excerpts from an 'Autobiographical Essay'" (*Jackson Advocate* 23–29 Feb. 1984: 2E), and his responses to my "Inquiry for the Eighties" questionnaire, dated 9 March 1984.

Autobiography and the attempts to give aesthetic shape to elusive aspects of a people's culture(s) are distinctive features of Plumpp's work. Literature, for Plumpp, is at once an act of creative intimacy with southern rural and Up-South urban cultures and one of forthright political articulation: the self cannot be "realized" without sustained examination of and negotiation with its specific histories. Yet, one does not have to know Plumpp's personal history to grasp the power of his work, since it maintains its integrity under sophisticated scrutiny. Nevertheless, biographical information helps to clarify some allusions; it illuminates the value of his recontextualizing patterns of folk life and thought; it helps us to "make sense" of Plumpp's thorough absorption and critique of the blues ethos. To be sure, such writers as Charles Chesnutt, James Weldon Johnson, Zora Neale Hurston, Richard Wright, and Amiri Baraka are forerunners in the literary tradition to which Plumpp has committed himself. Even so, his grounds and warrants are radically different from those of his literary ancestors and appreciating the more subtle textures and modalities of his work depends on knowing some facts about Plumpp the man and Plumpp the artist.

Talk Between the People and the Soil

Every black heart
hangs
petrified, mocked
by its own
indecision.

"From Gallows' Pole," *Portable Soul*

From "Autobiographical Essay"

I had inherited the legacy of slavery on tenant farms and had memorized its dictates. And I had skipped work in order to apprentice in the drawing room of petty bourgeois opportunity (for the uninformed that's what private Catholic colleges are). Whatever I had run from in faces tattooed by plantation tyranny met me in the Post Office. Everything in the P.O. seemed so biblical, primeval, inescapable. I committed my hands to work in the P.O. but withheld my soul. . . . I was afraid that the hell I had run from was mild compared to where I had wound up. I could not become an alcoholic crying: "If you crack the whip / I'll make the trip"; or some near-senile man walking thick-glassed and dragging eighty pound sacks for four decades; or a supervisor trapped behind a scheme making him a slave driver in the second half of the twentieth century. Therefore, I ran to whatever I could get depicting what writers saw in their worlds. At the time, I did not know whether I wanted to be a black writer or a white one, only that I wanted a vision fashioned from my experience and preserved by my skill.

Letter, 29 February 1984

Dear Sterling,

First, I am definitely reserving Saturday, March 17, for the interview, which my spirits tell me is going to be a pleasant experience for both of us. Instead of setting the questions now, I would prefer to deal with some broad areas that are essential to understanding you as a black man, as a Mississippian, and as a writer. The areas I will want to cover are: 1) your growing up in Mississippi, your high school and college years, and your perception of ancestry, much of which you have covered in your autobiographical pieces;

2) your participation in the Chicago phase of the Black Arts Movement, your work with OBAC, and your insights about the Chicago scene now; 3) your books of poetry, your prose and fiction, your editing, your winning the Carl Sandburg Award. . . .

Letter, 10 March 1984

Dear Jerry,

I am attempting to write responses to your concern about the interview; that way what's on my mind will not be forgotten. I was born January 30, 1940, the second child under my mother's maiden name, and I was reared by my grandfather and grandmother, until his demise in 1955. During my formative years, I was around old folks a lot—my grandfather was sixty when I was born and my grandmother was fifty—and we worked land for survival during the old man's declining health. My older brother Wardell Johnson was also born under my mother's maiden name. My grandfather was Victor Emmanuel and my grandmother's name is Mattie Emmanuel. I take it my grandfather was born under his mother's maiden name and that his real father was one John Peterson and that the midwife, also called godmother, named him after the reigning king of Italy. However, my brother and I were told who our natural fathers were and were introduced to their families before we could speak. My brother's father was Cutter Johnson and lived across the railroad tracks, and my father was Cyrus H. Plumpp who lived down the dirt road a piece. I cite this genealogy now because a great deal of the milieu surrounding me during my development hinged on this extended family and my awareness of it.

Victor Emmanuel was a patriarch without money. He made the decision and his word was the first and last. I have seen him slap grown children more than once for being too loose with their tongues with him. He was short, humpbacked to the side (as legend has it, when he was a child he was thrown by a horse and broke his collar bone and refused to tell his mother until it was too late for doctors to rectify his bone), black and walked with a little trot. His voice was deep and he possessed eyes designed to look through steel. My grandmother is peach, sweet, never reciting a harmful word or doing a harmful deed. I remember her washing dishes, digging in the flower beds in the front yard and hanging out clothes while singing "Do Lord, Do Lord, Do remember me." The good girl is ninety-four and going strong.

I had a very large sense of family at an early age. Further, I saw what it meant to be black, poor and have to work for white landowners. I saw an old grandfather barely eke out rent the last fourteen years of his life, and I saw him rearing his grandchildren as if they were his own, despite the fact that he was poor. I further heard what folks said to him and heard him say what happened to black folks if they spoke out of turn to whites to whom they were indebted. From my mother, aunts, uncles, and other people in their age groups, I heard the rituals of night life, the jokes, the lies about seeing ghosts and haints, and the desire to leave the tyranny and constraint of Mississippi and find some Promised Land where a day's wages were paid and the cycles of indebtedness would not continue endlessly. I also lived on the land and could fish, see snakes: moccasins, spreading adders, green snakes, joint snakes, black snakes, king snakes, and chicken snakes, and could bash their heads in with a stick I was taught to always carry. I could explore muddy ponds for fish and turtles, and pick berries and wild plums and grapes and muscadines and persimmons. Could go out in the woods, find pineknots and springs, hunt possums at night. I learned the tales about ghosts and haints and knew when old folks died and even saw the hearse come get them and take them to the funeral home (in those days there were no ambulances which would take individuals to hospitals and have them pronounced dead; the undertaker would be called and a hearse would come and take the body to the funeral home for embalming).

I grew up learning the mythology which black peasants in Mississippi had inculcated. I often heard the blues and saw adults move their bodies in ways which excited me. The terror I know about white folks was always in what I had heard they had done to somebody else and nothing was done in return. They drove trucks, big cars like a bat out of hell—down the dirt and gravel roads. They went to school in buses, past the fields we were working on. They drank coffee, ate toast, and relaxed in club cars as the passenger train from Vicksburg passed by the fields. I remember seeing Poppa (that's what we called my grandfather) stop, rear back on his plow, and look at the world of those dressed-up folk, look at the world as if to say it is passing me by. From the hot sun in fields I learned the tasks of unhitching mules and horses, taking them to water and feeding them, and coming to the house and washing up, eating and going back to the field, and working till sundown, and coming home and going through the same rituals, but only now hogs had to be slopped and fed. Often during periods when water was lean, one had to go long distances on foot to get water for baths, and the job of fighting off mosquitoes by spraying and burning rags taxed an already aching and dirty body. Many times only lye soap (soap made from grease, lye and ashes) or rough soap would be available to clean a body in a wash tub.

The first fifteen years of my life were dictated by the fear that loving and caring grandparents would die, and I would have to embark on the adventure of living with my mother and stepfather. They were the years which apprenticed me to the lore of black folks as I saw ex-slaves walking around on this earth, old, greyed, and barely moving one foot ahead of the other one, but living. I also learned the world black peasants in Mississippi were forced to live in: the shanty houses with tin roofs, sparse bricks uplifting them from the ground, and sliding shutters as windows; shanties which shook so seriously during storms when the lightning lit up everything and thunder almost shattered glasses that the old got on bended knee and asked the Lord to allow the storm to pass over and leave the house standing and the good souls in it alive and well. After the storms had passed, doors would be opened and the old would stand on porches (garries I believe we called them then) and talk in subdued tones as we watched the waters erasing fields and roads and heading downhill toward some stream or creek.

Interview, 17 March 1984

JERRY WARD: So you have to immerse yourself psychologically into what it was to live at that time. You seem to be telling me, Sterling, that if you go back to write about your ancestors, your people in the nineteenth century, you don't want to write about them as a historian. Or at least you write about them as a historian who is a participant.
STERLING PLUMPP: This is correct. I feel, whatever the chaos and disorder in my mind as I react to a specific kind of history, my experience has forced me to do a great deal of trekking into the past, into the roots, reflecting, introspecting, whatever words you like. I do a great deal of trying to find the psychological beat to the experience. I then try to develop language, paragraphs, and imagery to fit the beat. That is how I operate as a writer.

JW: If you identify psychological beat with the blues, you have to deal with several issues. The psychological beat for Americanized Africans is both secular and spiritual. The spirituals and other forms of sacred music and the seculars both, I think, are taproots for blues, gestalts. If you stop with the blues and minimize the tradition of popular music—ragtime, the rhythm and blues that got called soul, the new phenomenon of fusion—and jazz, what have you done in identifying the pulse of black culture? What is at issue is whether the musical pulse one identifies is correct for the background out of which one is writing. The blues might be right for an agrarian background, a Mississippi peasant background. It might not be right for other black experiences in America where jazzier forms operate. I think specifically of blacks in the East, or urban areas of the South, like New Orleans. Obviously, the mode is jazz, not blues.

SP: I think the basic self in Sterling Plumpp is blues, a kind of beat that gets transformed somewhat later into urban blues. I grew up hearing the spirituals and blues simultaneously, gospels and oral, chant-like praying, and the beautiful sermon being preached. No one writer can represent the totality of black experiences. My problem is to look for and develop a language out of the blues, because the blues is not static. There are aesthetic problems, depending on whether I am writing poetry or a novel or a play. It poses problems because often the repetition on the page destroys the natural statement and lyricism of the blues. You can't make the toughness and multilayered effect work. It comes off as if it is contrived.

JW: Yes, communication with your readers will depend much on details, not repetition, on what your words make us feel.

SP: I think I know whether the poem is working. I think I'm honest enough to know. In fact, when I wrote *Worst Than the Blues My Daddy Had*, I might have indicated to people I asked to read it that I did not think it was working. I will rely on readers. They narrow the possible ways a poem might work. You see, there are an infinite number of ways a poem might work. Readers help you zero in somewhat, if you are really honest when you view your work critically. I have no need to create work just to say it is out there. If it's not worthwhile, if it's not communicating, if it's not at the level at which the lives of black people have been for so many years in the world, there is no point in having the work published. I see myself as a beginner in the field of blues poetry. One of the problems I'm having has to do with autobiography. *The Mojo Hands Call, I Must Go* is highly autobiographical. The poems are autobiographical prophecies. When I deal with the blues, I have to deal with ancestral prophecy. I'm not sure I'm ancestrally specific enough.

JW: There aren't many models for what you want to do. The person who experimented most extensively with blues was Langston Hughes. I recall a criticism a blues player, Big Joe Duskin, made of Hughes's lyrics. He said, "They need correction." They were too literary, too artificial. They needed a certain connection with life. No woman sleeps with her mouth as wide open as a well. So, Duskin rewrote the lyrics. Some of the feedback might have to come from blues players.[2]

SP: In that sense I'm fortunate. SOB (Sons of Blues)/Chitown Hustlers recorded "Sons of Blues."[3] There is another poem set to be recorded and there's still another that I've written. They do tell me the words ought to be changed. I can't hear the music. The blues is more than lyrics; the blues is music, lyrics plus the music. I am a true worshipper at the shrine of the blues. I've religiously listened to the blues throughout my entire development. Even though I've been Catholic and have gone to middle-class schools, the music which always moved me has been the blues. Early during my life in Chicago, I'd go up on Homan to hear Muddy Waters, go over on Lake Street to hear Howlin' Wolf and I'd do the same thing over and over and over again. Except for the period when I discovered black culture, a great deal of it in the folksongs of Odetta, because she was singing the whole gamut. Not the voice, the lyrics of the songs.

JW: You mean she was going from blues to gospel, but she was also doing something else with black culture . . . it was black culture of the diaspora, not local in terms of being United States.
SP: It was diaspora. Odetta, Miriam Makeba, and Nina Simone forced me to deal with more folk culture than blues. But blues has been what I was interested in even before I was interested in writing. I thought I wanted to become a blues singer. I thought I would play the harmonica at one point. I thought I wanted to make my mouth make those sounds. But if one is a writer, one is stuck with the most basic experience of all—the survival in the church. For me, it is something with the psychological beat of the blues and something of the eloquence of the South. There's a southern black speech. It is not dialect, because often the vision is larger than what one associates with dialect.

JW: It has to do with our use of metaphor, turns of phrase, intonation. The South, black and white, seems to have a monopoly on that kind of narrative and speech. I want to ask why you said you had *discovered* black culture when you have always been *in* black culture.
SP: That has to do with my background. I was born in 1940 to a mother under her maiden name and I was the second child. My grandfather, who was born in 1880—sixty years before—did not believe in stepfathers. So he took me as his child. But he was also somewhat liberal. I was always told to carry the name of my father, my real father, though he had nothing to say about my life. I was in black culture—the praying, the baseball games, the hog killings, the eating of lights and the liver, the cleaning of chitterlings,

the making of the sausage, the dancing, the jokes, the lies they would tell about ghosts and haints they would see, how they would conjecture when they saw storms and pray when lightning would flash through the house and rattle the tin roof—I was born into that. At least two things happen coming up in White America, if one is a peasant, if one is dirty. You don't want the position of being poor. You don't want to be in the position of having to say "yassuh." And one's economic survival is dependent upon those kinds of behavior. I think subconsciously then I wanted books. I did not want to be white, for there was no way to be white. So, at the age of fifteen when I went to Holy Ghost Grammar School and later to Holy Ghost High School, I met a situation where all of the teachers were white, all of the students were black and a large number of them came from what was on paper or off the paper the black middle class. I was very bookish. A lot of the ritual of black life I was not immersed in. I love the music, but I didn't dance. I hardly danced at all. I was also very religious. I became a Catholic, which might have had something to do with my wanting to identify with the system that was educating me. Or of wanting to identify with some of those who were bringing enlightenment to me. The enlightenment had more to do with teaching me to read and to manipulate the symbols of the idols of capitalism than with God. On the other side, I was in a situation where my mother's marriage was breaking up, and she had a series of lovers whom I saw, and I had to actually throw papers to buy my clothes and pay my tuition. Coming home finding everything put out, having my life broken up and going to live with an aunt. The aunt is married to or is the common-law wife of a bootlegger. I knew a whole lot about the devil's work that went on in the business. So, I would clean up on Tuesdays and listen to Howlin' Wolf sing "Evil" or B.B. King, "Eyesight to the Blind," "Five Long Years." I had the culture, but that was not what I aspired to master. *I had it.* I could not run away from the culture. I was in the culture. So listening to Odetta sing "Hound Dog," listening to her talk about "Jack of Diamonds" or "Jesus Speak So Sweet, I Can Hear the Shuffle of the Angels' Feet" brought that world back to me and forced me, for a long period of time in Chicago, to go into restaurants and bars and to observe the way black people act and to listen to the way they talk. I wanted to be sure I had heard the way they talked whether I could write it down or not.

JW: I think your work is grounded in a very different way. You select from the vast repertory of black culture, connect with it autobiographically. Music and soil. I don't mean land. I mean the soil as a total experience for people who were first forced to deal with it and who later accepted dealing with it as a way of life, even after they were nominally free of doing so. Beyond acceptance to an understanding of importance, the earth as a life-giving gift for mankind. You select out the particular kinds of pain that black people have to suffer. Very often the pain of lying to the self. I recall your early poem "Lucille" about the "virgin" who had a child three days after her marriage, a blond child. That was a rich criticism of something fundamental in southern culture, the notion of morality. False morality. Young women do not have sexual experience before marriage, but everyone knows they are having sexual experiences. But they are not supposed to. And the girls put the guys off with "I'm not supposed to." The selectivity I find in your recent work, say in *The Mojo Hands Call*, taps into something Ishmael Reed has dealt with, the hoodoo as opposed to the voodoo tradition, hoodoo being very African American or United States. With *The Mojo Hands Call*, you have a spiritual return to Africa. The book was published the same year as your anthology, *Somehow We Survive*. Then, you had an earlier African connection, because Kgositsile wrote the preface for *Steps to Break the Circle*. So, how important has Africa been for you as a writer?

SP: I believe my sense of the poet as the historian of a people's total experience was reinforced a great deal by Kgositsile through his imagery. And the idea of the very long poem which is nothing but a series of lines extended, a series of short poems extended. Reinforced by Mongane Serote, the author of *No Baby Must Weep*, and enormously, enormously moved and influenced by Aime Cesaire, who may be the greatest living black poet in the world. But the work in *Somehow We Survive* is not so much a call to violence as a reliance on psychology. The writers' commitment is their psychology. South African writing moved me to look beyond the narrowness of what was called either the black aesthetic or Black Nationalism in this country in the 1960s. A great deal of that became premature for me. So I was forced to look at Afro-American culture the way Amilcar Cabral looked at the culture of Guinea-Bissau in *Return to the Source* and to conclude that if there were large numbers of Afro-Americans who did not have their culture, that was their fault.[4] We should look to those who do have it. On the question of Africa . . . I came up in Mississippi and have seen my uncles go out and buy rabbit feet and an assortment of ornaments and dust to sprinkle and cross "X" up the chimney to make sure that their women came back. So my blues connection is taken as ancestral autobiography and prophecy. Editing *Somehow We Survive* made me deal concretely with my own Africanity.

Once I saw the limitations of visioning myself as Mississippi and United States, I tried to create a larger stage.

JW: How large will that stage become? Does expanding your stage with the Mississippi blues mode . . . well, will your nonfiction, for example, embrace global issues from an African American perspective?

SP: Obviously, I will begin to write essays. There is a Palestinian poet, Mahmoud Darwish, who reads for forty or fifty thousand defeated Palestinians coming to Egypt from Beirut. Or he will read poems an hour long, or write a ten-page poem in a leading paper in Beirut to the invading Israeli soldiers. Here is a man who did not exist when he was coming up in Israel, because he was not supposed to be in the country. Obviously, he is denied his rights in his homeland. Many African writers have been driven out. Ngugi wa Thiong'o was jailed in Kenya for putting on a play.[5] The horrors of inhumanity extend well into black nations, into Haiti. Writers have disappeared in Guinea, in Ghana. They have been jailed and driven out of Algeria. I will look at those problems, at countries like Colombia, Nicaragua, Cuba to see if there is freedom of speech. I cannot assume speech is free. I am sympathetic toward the Cuban Revolution. I wonder though whether Cubans have freedom of speech, whether people are being oppressed when they are writing something patriotic. In poetry, I am writing a duo-epic poem, a split-page poem with a female voice on one side and a male voice on the other. The drafts of the poem, dealing with historical figures, force a consideration of black techniques, shifting from blues to spirituals to gospels to folk.

JW: What you want to do on the page is what one can do with split-screen film. It's damned effective. You want the male voice to jump out of its space into the female's space and vice versa. The experiment shows how daring you are, but some of these things just may not work. Not because you are incapable of writing it, but because you have not trained an audience how to read it.

SP: That's true. I had the problem of not knowing what the audience could receive in writing *Clinton*. At the time I was breaking with the tradition of my Chicago peers who were writing shorter, more urban poems. There was definitely a break by the time I got to *Steps to Break the Circle*. There was almost complete alienation from what they were doing by the time I got to "Fractured Dreams" and *The Mojo Hands Call*.[6] In many ways, the blues had become metaphysical. The perception of reality for the poet had become uncomfortable and disjointed. The writer still has to write until whatever he writes solves his own chaos. Chaos is a moving force for the Afro-American writer. That is why we have jazz. We improvise. For me, it is a lifelong experiment. I'm under no compulsion to create the epic poem in the next four or five or twenty years, but I would like to do the duo-epic in my lifetime. I suspect what I am doing in blues poetry and the blues novel will be the immediate object of my concern, trying to perfect and focus them, trying to devise a better technique and revise the material for publication.

From Worst Than the Blues My Daddy Had

My future as a poet is in the direction of the epic; this is the ultimate direction of my work, since the epic is the only form to present the many worlds Afro-Americans have undergone over the last four hundred years or so. In such an epic many legends, historical characters, and events could be handled, and the challenges of language and of improvising the epic form to suit an Afro-American tale would be great. I see myself as a vessel through which history flows: times past, events gone, and people gone speak with my voice. I love man, have made him the center of my world, and I will continue to sing his song.

Interview, 17 March 1984

JW: Although your development went against the grain of what your peers were doing in Chicago, it was consistent with earlier experiments in black writing.
SP: My experience in Chicago did not begin with OBAC (Organization of Black American Culture). There were at least two writing movements. I went to Chicago in 1960, worked at the Chicago Post Office between 1962 and 1969 and I was in the army, 1964–65. There is a key difference between some of us writers and the writers who emerged from OBAC. Many of us were writers who read before we wrote anything. We read and assessed everything—James Baldwin, Richard Wright, Dostoevsky, Albert Camus, Ralph Ellison, Jean Paul Sartre, Henry Miller, Arthur Miller. Reading, trying to understand how to make a statement, how to develop a technique. It was actually the army and the death of my father in 1965 that unlocked in me the precise articulation of what I felt so that I could write. One of the first complete poems that I wrote was about him, seeing his face dead and feeling the cold body, and going down this tenant road to St. Paul's Church and

going across the road and burying him. That experience stayed with me, and I tried to write. In the army, I read a lot. I was very immersed in Malcolm X and black books. I was alienated from absurd, New York intellectualism.

JW: How could you not deal with *the absurd* if you were reading Camus?
SP: I was dealing with existentialism. I thought that if you were black, you were existentialist.

JW: Richard Wright thought the same thing.
SP: Wright was the author of existentialism for me. The book that had the greatest impact was [Benjamin A.] Botkin's *Lay My Burden Down*. It moved me. I looked at the faces of those people in that book, and I saw the face of every old black person I had seen when I grew up. I was still trying to become articulate about my experience, jotting down poems and impressions, my reactions to the civil rights movement, Malcolm X's murder, King, Selma, Watts, Vietnam. And I knew people who were dying. All of this was pushing me to write. When I left the army, I was at the stage of rejecting literary analysis and of trying to make sense out of what people were actually doing.

From "Autobiographical Essay"

I became a writer the day I realized words had the meanings you gave them, had the life sucked from bones of your experience, had power if you freed them from lies.

Letter, 10 March 1984

I had been consciously writing or in the process of writing for seven years when the Organization of Black American Culture instituted its creative writing workshop in 1967. I had read Baldwin, knew the value and terror of aloneness for the creative. The steps up the dark ladders of discovery must be taken alone and in solitude. I remember reading a book a day often during those seven years, remaining awake twenty-four hours at the typewriter with only three incomplete sentences called up. I was also nearing the completion of a bachelor of arts in psychology and working full-time and reading and participating in Chicago CORE. James Cunningham was the first to tell me about OBAC and a writers' workshop which was meeting in the home of Gwendolyn Brooks. People were beginning to wear naturals.

I was busy going to various blues nightclubs and soul food places, listening to records, reading books, and trying to develop a poetic language. Originally, I told Cunningham I might be interested and procrastinated for a long time and eventually I heard about Don L. Lee who was a member of both workshops. Cunningham further informed me of the battle he was waging within OBAC for his own individual voice and about the attacks against him. He was pointing out what a new voice Don L. Lee was becoming and how the new atmosphere was breathing new life into his literary projects. I have always felt that James Cunningham possessed an exemplary critical mind and would make a major contribution to literature one day because of his talents.

I had a strong feeling at the time that this new black writing was serving the interests of those doing the promoting and defining more than it was serving the masses of black people or the writers themselves. . . . I felt, somehow, a game was being run on somebody. Fortunately, Don L. Lee agreed to publish *Portable Soul* and informed Hoyt Fuller about me. Hoyt wrote, inviting me to become a member of OBAC. I did in 1969.

Interview, 17 March 1984

JW: What preceded OBAC?

SP: It was basically the stage when a lot of young black intellectuals would read Baldwin, Ellison, James Joyce, Dostoevsky . . . discuss the reading; would listen to Bessie Smith, to blues, jazz, classical music . . . discuss it; would meet, go to all the used bookstores, collect black books; meet in the integrated places of Hyde Park (Oliver Twist, that's mainly where the black intellectuals congregated) and go to the blues nightclubs and talk about what they saw. This was happening between 1962 and 1967. There is no leader, but people are learning about literature. They don't know whether they are going to be black writers or Negro writers or what. They know that there is something in black literature, but if Baldwin is an outstanding writer—he is not white—he is writing about the black experience. That inspired many people in my generation. Debating over whether the Nation of Islam was correct, whether King was correct, discovering that Malcolm X and the Honorable Elijah Muhammad were really eloquent. They had come out of the black church and had taken it in a different direction. You see, this was a whole phase of studying and discussing Odetta and Nina Simone. The black riot, the urban riot which is activism, the people's. . . . Our example was in the activist movement. I, for example, was in CORE and marching and demonstrating. At that particular time, if you were in CORE and not in SNCC you were not revolutionary, and I had to deal with that. But I was into open housing and education. So that out of the response to the complete rejection . . . the language that was used by those who rebelled . . . the people who wanted to be writers had begun to imitate that urban language, so cool and dead. And many of those people gathered around Gwendolyn Brooks and Hoyt Fuller. Because there were overlapping groups. The first group was Haki Madhubuti (Don L. Lee), Walter Bradford, Carolyn Rodgers, Johari Amini, Kharlos Wimberli (who is now dead), Alicia Johnson, Mike Cook, Ebon Dooley. And a little later Barbara Mahone McBain. They would meet with David Llorens, Hoyt Fuller, and Abdul Akalimat (Gerald McWorter) and discuss things in terms of the new blackness. Hoyt sort of laid out the need for a new black aesthetic. At the same time, I think Cecil Brown and Sam Greenlee were there. So there was this new black thing and the need for new black critics. Haki and Carolyn Rodgers got some national attention because of their responses to Hoyt Fuller's questionnaire to new black writers.[7] I think maybe June Jordan, Ishmael Reed, and Alice Walker got attention also. They had some kind of credibility. At this time, OBAC had a speakers' bureau, so the names of OBAC writers were circulated until they got national exposure to the black studies programs and their exposure began to appear. This was coupled with the phenomenon of small black presses. So Haki, Carolyn Rodgers, and Johari Amini are some of the first in the Chicago area to have small black books. And then the Ellis Avenue bookstore, the Afro-Arts Theater. All these things reinforced one another. Those who had urban styles and very brilliant reading styles tended to get promoted quicker. They reached the limelight. In terms of exposure, there were at least two anthologies. There was the *NOMMO*, one and two, out of the OBAC Writers Workshop, *A Broadside Treasury* (Gwendolyn Brooks) and *Jump Bad* (Gwendolyn Brooks). So you see, there was this kind of activity. Moreover, those Hoyt Fuller felt were very good got poems published in *Black World.* Their work got reviewed in *Black World.* And I came to OBAC in 1969 through an invitation from Hoyt Fuller. I had manuscripts. I came in with *Portable Soul* (1967). The next year it was *Half Black Half Blacker.* Two years later it was *Black Rituals*, and two years after that *Steps to Break the Circle.* I published *Clinton* in 1976.

Fuller is the one who wrote the recommendation for me to get the job at the University of Illinois (Chicago Circle campus). He's the one who wrote the recommendation for me to become an assistant professor, he and George Kent. He's the one who got me a job at Voorhees College before I came up for tenure. It's a brilliant thing, if you are being promoted. But that does not mean you are the best exponent of the culture out there. It means that you can write and you might be completely alienated from the people. But as people's careers began to develop, there was no method of critiquing the limitations of their work. I mean people having five or six books before they are thirty years old. And at the same time other people are being told they are too European for the general climate now. And one of the most brilliant writers was not even allowed in the group—Amus Moore.

JW: Because the only people who recognized his genius were . . .
SP: A. B. Spellman.

JW: Yes, Spellman and Larry Neal.
SP: Moore was a brilliant writer, but he would not be a spokesman for the black aesthetic. He would be a brilliant poet. So it seems to me, Fuller was marketing writers, and the writers he marketed were legitimizing his idea of the black aesthetic. We were almost put into a box where we had to uphold the black aesthetic. Hoyt was not a good judge or a good critic of poetry. We would try to tell him that, but he would try to promote what he wanted to promote. He would give awards, like the Conrad Kent Rivers Award, based on his impressions. Maybe a couple of people deserved them, but I do not see how in the world some people got them. A lot of people didn't get these awards. Larry Neal didn't get one. Henry Dumas didn't get one. There's no logic to the formation. The role Hoyt played created a lot of psychological problems with other people. At one point, I began to think that if I remained in OBAC, I would have to fight Hoyt over the organization. And I did not think that was important. If an organization exists, and writers go to it voluntarily, that's a good thing. I don't think a writing workshop is a place to wage war. I told Hoyt that OBAC was not a liberation organization, that he should not tell people it was one. Then, in order to get jobs, OBAC people began to say that they were black. But they developed a kind of stance that would not alienate white people and would enable them to get jobs with arts councils. There was no commitment. I had gone the way of the university, so I left OBAC.

JW: What year did you leave?
SP: I left in 1972. I officially stopped going to meetings, but I never had anything against Hoyt or the organization. But younger people were coming into the organization, jockeying for position and grants became full-time

work, and I could not engage in that kind of thing. I don't call people for readings. I don't respond to book reviews. If I get a bad one, the only thing I wish is that the editor would have enough respect to pick someone literate enough to read my work. So, I left, and I don't think the definition of black aesthetic ever matured.

JW: Why?
SP: I don't feel that the writers talking about a "black aesthetic" in the 1960s knew a goddamn thing about it. I think that in the sixties many more writers created with the "intention" to promote a "black aesthetic" or to write for black people with an art derived from black culture. But if one examines any of the so-called "black aesthetician" writers of the 1960s, one finds they knew far less about black people than they did anything. What they wrote mimicked black folks at the surface level and dared not dive to any depths. There is still an intense investigation on the part of black writers into black life which necessitates that a new far-seeing eye be brought to culture and the possibility of a black audience. Many black writers still promote the essence of a "true black aesthetics," but they would not dare allow the phrase "Black Aesthetics" to be used to describe what they are attempting. That's something I couldn't articulate when I was in OBAC. I began to move in a new direction, forming relationships with blues singers and going to blues clubs. What has happened with OBAC since Hoyt Fuller left *Black World* is that Angela Jackson has tried to hold the organization together and to carry on the tradition. But Angela is not Hoyt. She does not have the contacts that Hoyt had with those in powerful decision-making positions, positions that affect people's careers.

JW: It would seem that Angela Jackson represents the end, the futile effort to keep OBAC alive.
SP: The social milieu for OBAC has changed; therefore, OBAC is seeking a new identity in a changing world.[8]

JW: So we arrive at the sad 1980s: Chicago is a very interesting place that has nothing to say. The New York side of everything had disintegrated as far as black people were concerned, and the only places anything was going on was in the South and the West. What do you see as the future of Chicago in terms of black writing?
SP: I think the politics of the movement dictated to writers what they could say before they had consciously studied craft. There was never any attempt

on the part of the black aesthetic movement in Chicago to force the society to accept black writing on its own terms. Writing had to be "relevant." People now find themselves trying to get to know who one needs to know to get published as opposed to their sitting down and writing and trying to figure out what is the culture, what are the directions of our lives, what is the beat, what beat will I have to discover to have my voice. If more people did that, it would be a healthy situation. Because Chicago has a black mayor, you have an artificial consciousness, and this artificial consciousness works to the disadvantage of people who have to perceive poor people. Electoral politics helps middle-class black folks. It may help other black folks psychologically, but the fact of the matter is that if Jesse Jackson gets a lot of votes in Mississippi and you get a Democratic president, some person from Mississippi will get a large chunk of money from the Small Business Administration. And if you are poor and on welfare in Mississippi you will still be there when the election is over. So, the idea of having it made narrows the perception of the writer. Chicago writers are not attentively looking at Nicaragua, Cuba, South Africa, Palestine. Chicago writers have technique. They need to say something. Like what does it mean to be black and a serious writer?

JW: Let us come back to Mississippi. How does anyone growing up black in Mississippi get to be brilliant?

SP: When I moved from the country with the opportunity to go to school full time, I was also like a Booker T. Washington—not having a name and trying to get a new start. I was two years older than most of the students and had been to school less time than they had. I had never been to school more than three months out of a year. I devoured books and was blessed with a retentive memory. I was very quick of mind. I could read a math book and learn how to solve the problems, whether calculus or plane geometry. I have a graphic memory for mathematics. Yet, I had to close myself off from obstacles. I had to sacrifice a social life. I was religious, so much so that I almost became a priest. I didn't drink or smoke. I was at home every night before dark if I wasn't playing basketball. I didn't go to the Four O'clock Tearoom or Steven's Rose Room. That's how one becomes brilliant. Some people make the mistake of thinking mind power is a matter of class, of what your parents can do for you. Class cannot make you appreciate and want knowledge. Knowledge was what I wanted. There was a middle-class black world in Jackson [Mississippi] that shut me out. I was determined they would never whip me at anything. They would be taught a lesson, an academic lesson. I'd be right there when the other students graduated.

JW: Sterling, I think the barriers put up by the black middle-class are extremely fragile. To a great degree, black middle-classness rests on intellectual achievements. So anyone who is able to excel intellectually can get in.
SP: Well, you can. But what happens during the formative teenage years? Dating, parties, having access to cars, a free teenage life? I never had that. I think you are in academically, and they can't put you out. They will not attack you. But because of my condition, I came to hate that society. I came to the conclusion that my father was the way the world was structured, period. I wanted to be brilliant, but there were so many things I did not want to be a part of.

Letter, 10 March 1984

In high school, I could not dance and had no permanent relationships with girls, but I could study and study I did. The nuns helped me a great deal, and I owe much of my academic success to them. I owe a great deal of my sanity to them because they were kind to me when I was in a state of turmoil internally. I once inquired formally about entering the seminary to become a priest, and I remember being told that the bishop would have to grant a letter of dispensation since I was born outside of wedlock. I feel my whole infatuation with becoming a priest stemmed from my need then to escape some fate—I wanted to be safe and thought vows of poverty, obedience, and celibacy and a lifetime of service to the Church would gain me that safety.

I became acutely aware of race in 1957 with the entrance of black students in Little Rock. It had more impact than the Montgomery bus boycott had had, because of the defiance of Faubus and the troops and the faces of those brave black souls walking with troops to make this democracy work. I also remember feeling threatened by Khrushchev when he came to this country and pounded on the table at the UN with his shoes and had his countrymen put Sputniks up in space.

I must also say that what permeated the inner sanctums of the soul of all black boys coming up with me in Jackson was fear, a fear so dreadful that no one ever spoke about it. It was a fear stemming from the realization that we, like Willie McGhee, Emmett Till, and Mack Charles Parker, would one day be burned up electrically, battered to death and tossed into the river, or taken from some jail and murdered—because of *her*, because someone said we had violated the white woman. This was the gnawing in the souls and consciousness of many black boys; many were destroyed by it and many studied to overcome its possibility. The sit-ins were beginning by my senior year in the fall of 1959, and we were aware of a new world approaching. I did not do exceptionally well on the National Merit Scholarship Test. I did, however, take a test at Jackson State and did so well that I was offered a four-year, all-tuition and all board scholarship. Saint Benedict's College in Atchison also offered me an all-tuition paid four-year academic scholarship. My scores on the standardized test hurt me, and I rejected Jackson State because I had not been counseled to accept it, and I went to Saint Benedict's in Kansas.

I arrived at college in the fall of 1960 with an all-tuition paid scholarship and no money for room and board. My aunt had to hastily send the amount in excess of $300 and I was given a job by the Dean of Students, Father Bede, a job sweeping the Administration Building and later cleaning up Saint Joseph's Hall where I lived. It was an all-male, mostly white liberal arts college, drawing heavily from the farm regions of Missouri, Iowa, Kansas, and from urban centers—Kansas City, St. Louis, Wichita, and Topeka. There were seven black students out of a total of approximately one thousand; two freshmen, Leodies Robinson, a star football player, and myself. The blacks were mainly from Kansas and Memphis. Across town at Mount Saint Scholastica, there were two black women out of a total of seven or eight hundred. I was the only black living in Saint Joseph Hall under the very stern and arrogant Father Joseph Conrad. He demanded compliance with the college rules and was very fair and supportive. I did exceptionally well in my first year, making the Dean's list. Perhaps my greatest achievement came in English where I made an "A" from Father Gervase, who was very frail and demonstrative in his actions. My chief problem at Saint Benedict's was how to pay for the room and board and have spending money. During the summer, I went to Chicago and could not find a job except for one or two days washing dishes. The fall of 1961 found me back at Saint Benedict's, moving off campus to live with Stephen Boone (first black student body president) in the home of an old black woman who charged us thirty-five dollars a month. I continued to clean floors and offices for my spending money, and I borrowed $1000 from the National Student Defense Loan. My sophomore year caused me to want to learn more about life, and I began drinking beer, playing cards, and reading on my own. I also discovered James Baldwin in a literature course. The story was "Sonny's Blues." From the moment I read Baldwin, I knew that my life would never be the same again. I did well in my sophomore year but did not make the honor roll. I began to see the differences between the way whites treated one another and the way they treated us. I began to make interesting discoveries about history in college.

Interview, 17 March 1984

JW: What did you find out?

SP: I began to discover a lot about atrocities against people in the New World who were here before the coming of the Europeans, and in particular about the enslavement of black people. I found out about Bartolome de Las Casas, who persuaded the pope to issue the *asiento*, to permit the importing of slaves by Spain and Portugal, about the barbarity of it all. I was reading these cold histories. Reading taught me . . . that I, in fact, was a fool. That way I discovered Richard Wright, Ralph Ellison, Langston Hughes, William Melvin Kelly, LeRoi Jones, James Weldon Johnson, W. E. B. DuBois, Booker T. Washington, Jean Toomer and *Cane*, Melvin Tolson. That way I actually began to read black literature.

I discovered E. Franklin Frazier, who had an enormous impact in helping me to understand history, the history of the Negro family and of the Negro church. I discovered Melville Herskovits's *The Myth of the Negro Past*. I began to try to piece back together this puzzle of who I am. And James Baldwin helped me to deal with the phenomenology of my own experience. And Richard Wright helped me to uncover the psychological perception one gets from facing the horror that I faced in Mississippi. He sharpened that kind of perception.

JW: As only Richard Wright could?

SP: Right. He heightened that kind of perception. He had a hypnotic effect on me. At that time I did not know I wanted to be a poet. I knew I wanted to write. I knew I wanted to create a particular vision of the world that my past had given me a vantage to see. I wrote fragments of poems. I listened to music a great deal. At some point, all of this synthesized and I tried to write poetry. Much of that poetry culminated in my attempt to be elliptical in my expression, to be sparse with quick rhythm and quick imagery. Not imagery of the absurd but imagery of the black experience. A great deal of that resulted in *Portable Soul*. Also, trying to give multiple meaning to words by the way they are placed on paper, so that linguistic as well as rhythmic experiences occur. But my own feeling is that *Portable Soul* is philosophical. At that point I had begun to play the black base.

JW: The language and craft were not there?

SP: Neither one was there. By the time I came to *Half Black Half Blacker*, I had remembered a great deal of what I had heard, seen, and felt. I had consciously begun to incorporate the folk in my work. Also the language was far more compressed. Tight imagery. I was changing. I never thought I was a black priest. I called that book *Half Black Half Blacker* to indicate a different level of perception within myself. The book that really made me become the writer was *Black Rituals*. What has to be noted is that I began *Clinton* in 1970. It was a difficult poem. In fact, I did not know how to write it. I wrote a poem called "Metamorphosis" that appeared in *Black World* in which I begin when I was ten (I was happy then) and wind up when I'm thirty.[9] The poem was written in 1970. Clinton was growing with me, but *Black Rituals* . . . I could not understand how one could deal with psychology without dealing with experience. The things that were at the core of experience for me were a strong grandfather and a very beautiful and supportive, arbitrating, religious, and spiritual grandmother. So that forced me to deal with a lot of the rituals, a lot of the strength of the experience that I was ashamed of subconsciously when I was becoming educated. I returned spiritually to the South with *Black Rituals*. The following year I dealt with the symbolic trek not of an individual but of the Movement, because the Movement moved from the South, which symbolized the young boys. It moved from Alabama to Chicago. And by the time Black Power came up, the Movement was still better in the South. And by the time it seemed we were getting black capitalism in the North, the opportunities were still in the South.

JW: A neo-carpetbagger philosophy.

SP: It was a neo-carpetbagger kind of philosophy, so that the black experience was dealt with symbolically, I thought. Experience in *Steps to Break the Circle* is autobiographical and symbolic. Much of the mode of folk experience—blues, gospel, sermon, language, diction—is there. My ear had learned the black song at last in *Steps*. *Clinton* represented a break in the sound barrier, because there I was able to capture both the imagery and the rhythm of experience. It was the first time that the saturated, rural, southern Clinton experience came forth in terms of imagery, metaphor, movement, the grandfather. It was hard times with affirmation. Music. And it moves from the "I," from the self back to the culture. That was *Clinton* and the mid-seventies. What was ahead for me in the eighties became apparent in two poems, at least. What I saw happening to myself as an individual if I only perceive myself in the urban definition of black nationalism, is represented in the poem "Fractured Dreams." Schizoid. It's uncertain. It's eerie. It's a damn surreal kind of experience to me. The path of clarity is partially represented by the history. "I Hear the Shuffle of the People's Feet" represents the collective "I," the movement from the slave ships until the dancing in the streets. So there was something of the sixties that was of value, the dancing in the streets.

JW: More than dancing in the streets, I hope.

SP: More than dancing in the streets, there was the discovery of self. It was not the dancing. It was not the riots. It was what they symbolized, the kind of determination that made Nat Turner, Frederick Douglass, and Louis Armstrong. You see, it symbolized that for me.

JW: The determination that made Sterling Plumpp . . .

SP: That made Sterling Plumpp. But the other aspect is that the poetry of the 1980s was also coming in. It was *The Mojo Hands Call, I Must Go*, what I call the taking of the spiritual, the African spirituality that existed for me when I grew up . . . the attempt to take it back to Africa . . . that is hoodoo. It is the images of mojo and hoodoo (which was real) that I use to describe the Africanity of all of us. That is what ultimately beckons me. But I cannot even go to that unless I accept my brother. Unless I accept myself in the pit. So, what I see for the 1980s is a complex vision. Obviously, the question of craft becomes important, because the challenge of trying to simply state blackness as I did in *Portable Soul* was not the craft of trying to evoke the experience in terms of folk that I tried in *Half Black Half Blacker*. The muted, compressed language of that book will not meet the challenge of the mind trying to narrate this odyssey, the movement of black people one finds in *Steps to Break the Circle*. And the sound, the rich sound, the all-pervading sound of *Steps* was not adequate to equate this threatening awareness of a larger world which destroyed the innocence of experience in *Clinton*. This harsh world being overcome by a discovery of self. The language of *Clinton* prepared me to deal with the successive stages. But my vision has changed again, because I have to deal with the fact that at the core of my experience *I am a southern writer*. The beat of my life is blues. The question is how to handle it. It is there as an experience, as a philosophy, and I am trying in my current writing to work it out. I attempted to work it out within traditional recorded blues form . . .[10]

JW: Which failed . . .

SP: No. It did not work. I am trying to capture it in a narrator narrating the experience of the people he is talking to in the novel, *Mighty Long Time*.

That creates many more problems. I will work with them in the novel. The basic different beats—be they blues, gospel, or jazz—those individuals find themselves in a particular corner. In the 1980s, that has to be worked out in poetry and drama. There has to be a much larger view of the poet as a master of the sound and imagery that relates to the folk, that captures but is not limited by the perceived notion of what the folk is. That is the direction of Afro-American literature, as I see it, for the next twenty years. That will lead to epic. You will have to deal with epic form.

JW: Yes, but will audiences read epic?

SP: Well, it is an enormous challenge. I think that more honest novelists, who are not trying to prove they have taken every graduate course or writers workshop in the world, will try to tell that story. For me, it is the blues singer. The blues singer represents something germane. It could have been the preacher. How does one become a preacher? That is why I am telling you where we must go. We should get back to the folk in a more searching way. A writer revives language, retranslates language. He resuscitates it. A blues novel will revive the elegance of the blues tradition. It will resuscitate it. It will take it from Chess records or wherever.

From "Autobiographical Essay"

No writer ever consciously becomes anything except an artist capable of expressing his deepest longings within the bosom of a select vocabulary. And it is precisely this question of meaning, searched-for definition, truce with reality, or redefinition—no matter what you call it—the meaning one arrives at in becoming an artist acts as a solar force to his psyche; therefore, any maneuver to tamper with it threatens the very gestalt of his soul. Thus, when the question of the relationship the black, oppressed writer bears to the revolutionary movement constructed to free his people is posed, I undergo the incredible metamorphosis of delay; I fall victim to fear, because the effort demanded to shape my vision was wine squeezed from a stone. The precious few satisfactions I have known stem from my discovery that somewhere within layers of my experience lay my tongue and the keys to my future. Therefore, it is no easy or simple task for me to unravel the artist in me from the politician in me. And this is the core of it: my lifelong climb to vision and mastery of expression may very well need the pruning hands of change.

Notes

1. "Strange Fruit." Rev. of *Blues: The Story Always Untold*, by Sterling D. Plumpp. *American Book Review* Jan.–Feb. 1990: 17, 24.

2. Steven C. Tracy. "A MELUS Interview: Big Joe Duskin." *MELUS* 10:1 (1983): 65–85.

3. Billy Branch composed the music for and performed Plumpp's poem, "Sons of Blues," on *Where's My Money?*, Red Beans, RB 004, 1984. Plumpp also wrote the liner notes for this album.

4. See especially Cabral's lectures, "National Liberation and Culture" and "Identity and Dignity in the Context of the National Liberation Struggle," *Return to the Source*, ed. Africa Information Service (New York: Monthly Review P, 1973): 39–69.

5. For details on this case and on the repression of African writers, see Ngugi wa Thiong'o, *Detained: A Writer's Prison Diary* (London: Heinemann, 1981) and *Barrel of a Pen: Resistance to Repression in Neo-Colonial Kenya* (Trenton: Africa World P, 1983). Plumpp's poem, "After Reading *Detained*," *Black Nation* 4.1 (1984): 57, provides a capsule of his thinking about political articulation.

6. The original version of "Clinton" appeared in *The Savage* (Winter 1975): n.p. It was substantially reworked and expanded for publication as a Broadside Press chapbook. "Fractured Dreams" appeared in *Another Chicago Magazine* 3 (1978): 53–62; the first version of "The Mojo Hands Call, I Must Go" in *Another Chicago Magazine* 4 (1979): 57–69. James Cunningham provides a most useful explanation of Plumpp's artistry in "Baldwinian Aesthetics in Sterling Plumpp's *Mojo* Poems," *BALF* 23.3 (1989): 505–18.

7. See *Negro Digest* 19.1 (1969): 4–36, 80–82.

8. For other views of OBAC's history, see *NOMMO: A Literary Legacy of Black Chicago (1967–1987)*, ed. Carole A. Parks (Chicago: OBAHouse, 1987).

9. "Metamorphosis (for Bro Yakie)," *Black World* 20 (June 1971): 17.

10. Plumpp refers to the early typescript (c. 1983) of his most recent collection of poems, *Blues: The Story Always Untold* (Chicago: Another Chicago P, 1989). He abandoned the derivative imitation of classical blues lyric that did not work in favor of modernist lyrical forms.

Interview with Blues Poet Sterling Plumpp

Toni Costonie / 1990

From *Jam Sessions* 4.10 (June 1990): 8–9. Reprinted by permission of the author.

Squeezed into a small concrete space, the kind that never lets you forget that you are in an "institution," in the University of Illinois at Chicago's Behavioral Science building is the office of African American literature professor Sterling Plumpp. Plumpp has been an associate professor for eighteen years. He has also written seven books of poetry. His walls are covered with posters and flyers from the Free South Africa movement, announcements of poetry readings, and other interesting memorabilia. The walls are lined with books of poetry, black literature, and history.

As he talks the concrete walls seem to disappear into the distance and a Free Africa poster, with a raised fist of defiance, the shackle and broken chain are still attached, as it reaches for the sky and blood trickles down the arm, seems to dominate the room.

Toni Costoni: You are a professor here?

Sterling Plumpp: I am an associate professor of African American studies. Currently papers have been prepared for me to be jointly appointed to the English Department. I was originally appointed in the English Department, in order for the program to grow when we didn't have any budget lines. That means that you had to have a unit and you had to more or less win your stripes; this was about 1972. Now that I am tenured as an associate professor we are trying to develop a graduate program in the study of African American life; it is in our interest to jointly appoint all of the professors.

TC: You have a recent book?

SP: My recent book is called *Blues: The Story Always Untold* and it is significant to me for a number of reasons. First, I am a Mississippian, I came out of an oral tradition, I was reared by a grandfather and a grandmother, born in 1880 and 1890 respectively. My grandfather died in 1955; my grandmother is still living at the age of one hundred. Blues to me represents a number of things: it is a language, it is a history, it is ancestry, it is music, it is lyric, it is mood, it is an attitude. All of that pertains to the way the Africans, or the descendants of those original Africans who came over on slave ships, tried to maintain some kind of psychic health in this New World. To me it was a kind of ritual that was performed to get rid of something that was very undesirable in the life of an African American.

TC: Kind of like purging yourself.
SP: Cleansing, a cleansing ritual.

TC: Did you grow up on the blues?
SP: I grew up listening to hard time prayers by my grandparents. I heard it on the gramophone and I heard it on the radio, Ernie's Record Mart from Nashville, Tennessee, and somebody from Del Rio, Texas . . . late late hours you could hear it. It was also the popular music on the jukeboxes and on black radio at the time, somewhere between 1948 and 1960. It was the music I had in mind when I thought of black music.

TC: Did you grow up in Mississippi?
SP: The first twenty years of my life were spent in Mississippi.

TC: Where?
SP: The first fifteen were spent outside of Clinton, Mississippi, on a cotton plantation; the next five years were spent in Jackson.

TC: Were your grandparents sharecroppers?
SP: They were sharecroppers.

TC: Where were your parents?
SP: Due to a variety of reasons my mother and father never married. My mother had another son; she never married his father. My grandfather took us over when we were born and reared us as his sons. He didn't believe in stepfathers.

TC: So you were raised in the true old black southern tradition?
SP: Old time . . . patriarchal grandfather.

TC: How did you wind up in Chicago?

SP: Beginning around 1944, or thereabouts, one of my aunts eventually left and came up, then came back in about 1951 and brought up her brother, in 1952 brought up the other brother, about 1956, or thereabouts, brought up a nephew, about 1957 brought up another nephew. I went to college in Kansas. When I dropped out temporarily, this was the place where I had family.

TC: What did you do when you first came to Chicago? How did you end up teaching?

SP: Actually when I graduated from high school, I won an academic scholarship to St. Benedict's College. After two years I dropped out and came to Chicago. I was fortunate enough to get a job as a clerk at the Chicago Post Office. I was in the army in '64 and '65, returned to civilian life at the beginning of '66, got a degree at Roosevelt University, and went to graduate school there for two years. However, I was becoming a writer at the same time so that by the time I had been at Roosevelt two years, I had published two short books: *Portable Soul* and *Half Black Half Blacker*. I had done the first chapter of the book called *Black Rituals*.

TC: *Portable Soul?*

SP: *Portable Soul* was the first book I wrote, *Half Black Half Blacker* was the second, 1969 and '70, Third World Press. That was at the time black studies was being set up. I had been reviewing books for *Black World* for about five years. I was editor at Third World Press and I was managing editor at *Black Books Bulletin* and my work had been anthologized in *The Poetry of Black America*, so I was fortunate enough to come in based on credentials at that time.

TC: How many books have you published?

SP: I think this is the eighth title. In 1969 I published a small book of poetry called *Portable Soul*, in 1970 I published another chapbook called *Half Black Half Blacker*. In 1971 I published a poem on a broadside called *Muslim Men*. In 1972 I published a collection of essays called *Black Rituals*. In 1974 I published one long poem as a chapbook *Step to Break the Circle*. In 1976 I published another long poem titled *Clinton*. In 1982 I had two titles. I edited a volume of South African poetry and short stories, *Somehow We Survive*, and my volume of poetry, *The Mojo Hands Call, I Must Go*, came out. In 1988 I was an associate editor of a book that came out on South African literature from the University of Chicago Press called *From South Africa*. In 1989 *Blues: The Story Always Untold* came out.

TC: Where did you get the title for *Blues: The Story Always Untold* from?
SP: I don't think the concept is mine. Larry Neal, an outstanding black critic and poet, did the book *Hoodoo Hollerin' Bebop Ghosts*. Larry Neal said when black people came across the Atlantic they brought a blues god with them. He also said that the blues represents ancestry, it is cyclical. Realizing that, I just knew that what I was doing is basically telling Sterling Plumpp's blues, or part of it; the story is so large that you cannot possibly attempt to tell it all. I got the concept from Larry Neal and I just sort of capsulized it.

TC: Last year, or maybe it was the year before last, we talked a bit when you were just getting back from Australia. Can we talk a little about that? I think that is something critical; we forget that part of the world is part of the African diaspora too.
SP: I was a writer in exchange with the state of New South Wales. A number of Australian writers had come to Illinois, and a number of writers from Illinois went to New South Wales. I was the only African American writer to go to Australia. No black Australian writer came here. I was curious. I don't know anything about aboriginals. When I asked questions, nobody knew how many there were. Recently, like in the last ten days, I received the first literary study of aboriginal writing. It is very shocking. When Captain Cook came in 1788, I understand there were about 300,000 aboriginals; in the 1920s there were as few as 40 or 50,000 aborigines; today in 1990 out of a population of 16 million they are 2 percent, that makes them somewhere between 250 thousand to 700 thousand. The first aboriginal to write a book in English was in 1929. The first aboriginal to write a book of poetry was in 1964. The first aboriginal to write a novel in English was in 1965. There is one aboriginal in the country with a PhD degree.

TC: What happened to them?
SP: I have to get you the book. They had a policy of trying to destroy their "primitive" way of life. The policy mandated that they would drown them in the white race. Black women were mated with white men and the children were taken away from the black mothers to be reared by white families. The children reared by these white families were trained to be maids or horsemen or cowboys. Unlike African Americans they become whiter; their

genes were recessive with respect to whites. There are a number of titles. The poetry and the drama seem strongest. I have about fifty titles of books that I brought back. I think I will probably donate them to this university and ask them to write other institutions so people can see. They ought to go into a research library where you can go there and see because they are very few.

I'm also going to ask this university for their support to get the complete collection of aboriginal works, so that somebody can come here and study for a master's and the resources would be here.

TC: What was your experience like there?

SP: It was almost like being, in some ways, invited to a lynching when a lynching was not taking place. They did not speak intelligently about aboriginal people. In other words, aboriginals have not forced their way on the imagination the same way we have. So getting information is like pulling teeth. For instance, ask how many aboriginals are there, they hem and haw; how many aboriginals have PhDs, they hem and haw; how many millionaires do they have?

TC: Are there any?

SP: I don't think so.

TC: They are poor people?

SP: The way they are forced to exist, a lot of them are on same kind of state subsidy. Most of them live in small towns. If you don't have a degree, how can you be an accountant or an engineer? If you can't get an education, how do you become an accountant or an engineer? They are very wealthy in terms of their culture; they are very lovely people.

TC: How long did you stay there?

SP: I was there for eleven days. I met some of the leading writers and one of the leading actresses there. In fact she has called me from Australia. My plan is to try to set up some mechanism so a delegation of Americans, with a large representation of African Americans, could go down there in some kind of dialogue exchange and we could bring out some of the art. The art is some of the best in the world.

TC: What was the rest of Australia like? Being there and being black, it is not supposed to be very friendly . . . in fact we can't get permanent visas.

SP: I was a guest of the state so it was deceptive.

TC: You got royal treatment?

SP: They went out of their way to make sure I didn't get embarrassed. Clearly they are not used to black people speaking their minds and saying what they think. You know rejecting things, saying I don't give a damn what you think. It is not the heritage of Nat Turner; that is my heritage, not theirs. Africa had a great heritage. It is an entirely different relationship. It is a very beautiful country, unpopulated beaches, a lot of outdoor life. The city is more humane because people live in downtown Sydney. They don't live in downtown Chicago. Seventy-five percent of the population lives in four cities, Brisbane, Sydney, Adelaide, and Melbourne. Very supportive of art, very supportive, three or four hundred people coming out for book parties and things like that. I was very impressed with everything except how the aborigines were treated. There didn't seem to be any reason since they only represent 2 percent of the population, if you give them a vote. Why discriminate against them? They don't have enough power to affect the lives of whites.

TC: They can't vote?

SP: They got to vote for the first time in 1967. They were counted in the census for the first time in 1985.

TC: That is rough. Is it close to the equivalent of South Africa?

SP: In some ways worse because it is hidden; no one knows about it. They don't have the Mandelas and these people who went to Harvard and know how to propagandize.

TC: Basically they don't have any strong leadership from within themselves?

SP: They have strong leadership but it is a question of numbers, it is a question I suppose of communication skills. Martin Luther King, W. E. B. DuBois, those people had PhD degrees. In other words, they understood propaganda of the West, and they had earned their credentials to fight in the arena. The aborigines haven't; they can't fight in anthropology and archaeology; they only have one PhD degree. If you had one hundred with PhD degrees, they would begin to attach what these anthropologists have said, you see. You are actually looking at them through the eyes of someone else.

TC: Is their travel restricted?

SP: I didn't get that impression, I think their capital is the basic way they are controlled. They don't have enough money to wage certain kinds of propaganda struggles. They are not a violent people. By nature they are not violent.

TC: They are not fighters?
SP: It is almost like, I don't want to say monks, they have a certain relationship to land; they were not people who tried to hold onto a thing; they said they belonged to the land.

Blue Verses: An Interview with Sterling Plumpp

Michael Antonucci / 2001

From *Obsidian III: Literature in the African Diaspora* 3.2 (Fall/Winter 2001–2002): 99–112. Reprinted by permission of the author.

This interview was recorded on the campus of the University of Illinois at Chicago, in Sterling Plumpp's office on the twelfth floor of University Hall on September 26, 2001. It was just after Professor Plumpp had made local headlines through a bit of luck with an Illinois Lottery scratch ticket and a few weeks before his retirement at the end of the 2001 fall semester. He was typically thoughtful and candid.

Michael Antonucci: After your recent good fortune, there are a few lines that I pulled out of *Blues Narratives* which someone could use to hold your feet to the fire, but I am going to skip all that . . . (laughter). Going back to the questions I sent to you over the summer, we might begin with the one about church and family: The institutions of church and family figure prominently in your work from *Black Rituals* (1972) to *Blues Narratives* (1999). Would you care to speak about the central position that these tropes occupy within your corpus?

Sterling Plumpp: I think that the boundaries of my world, both vertically and horizontally, have a great deal to do with family. And much of this stems from the fact that I grew up standing on the shoulders of my grandparents who reared me, looking beyond my mother's generation and looking right back into the face of slavery because my grandparents had been born in 1880 and 1890, respectively. Their concept of squeezing meaning and hope through the prism of the God of their religion is something that stayed with me spiritually.

On the other hand, a great deal of what I came to understand as blues, I had initially witnessed in their tones and their expressions—the subdued

43

tones of how they talked about trouble, the celebratory tones of how they thanked God for letting them live another day. So a great deal of my language came from them.

But most importantly they were individuals who never had material possessions beyond that which was necessary to keep body and soul together and be considered human when they went into public in terms of clothing. Yet, within their lives there was a great deal of celebration. That always meant a lot to me. I cannot understand how things, even money, could make somebody important. Somehow I wanted to read the barometer of the souls of people; I think that I came to read the barometer of the souls of my grandparents. This was my initial education.

Church is a little bit more complex. Though I was apprenticed into the Baptist church, sitting on a mourner's bench doing revival and having somehow endured a two-to-three week tenure there, I felt that I had a sign which comes from the belief within this religious context that one had to have a conversionary experience before one was saved. I had felt that though I could not describe a star moving, that somehow there had been communicated to me a "feeling." So I indicated that I wanted to be baptized. I was baptized in a lake and joined this community of the church in a right hand of fellowship ceremony where I met every member of the church and my name was put on the church roll.

Now obviously a great deal of religion was taking place; to put it in the words of the people at church, "I had somehow found my way to the King's Highway." But for me, more importantly, I had found my way to a gathering where what was prized and praised was the eloquence of the brilliant speakers and singers. That is the influence; it was a power housed in the metaphoric power of the black preacher; the exultation and incantatory remarks and urgency in his threats and ridicules to his congregation. On the other hand, no matter how low my spirit was to fall there was something in the lyricism of the Negro spirituals and gospel music that lifted me up again.

Antonucci: You bring up the 1880s and this generational split that existed between you and your grandparents and the impact they have had on your vision and perspective. Your life experience, coming from the Deep South, effectively cuts across two generations. How has it shaped your relationship with black artists working in your generation? I'm thinking of your relationship with OBAC (Organization of Black American Culture) in the 1960s. Did this background produce a kind of tension for you?

Plumpp: The tension was precisely this: By the time that the Black Arts Movement in Chicago began and OBAC began in 1967, I had been seriously studying black literature since 1962 and literally imbibing every word Baldwin had ever penned; I had read Ellison, I had read Wright; I had read Hughes and McKay. I had read DuBois; I had read E. Franklin Frazier . . . [I saw that] a great deal of what was being forecast as blackness was expression that came from the urban vernacular; what was becoming deified as authentic African American culture was John Coltrane. I find it interesting that Louis Armstrong and Charlie Parker were not the examples. Trane is a great musician, but when I asked my friend Fred Anderson about the ARCM, he said, "Well, Plumpp, most of them cats take the late Trane, but I always catch the early Bird."

In other words, I was always suspicious of how much one knew about African American culture if one did not look at it through blues and the African American church. I was particularly suspicious of those who talked about Africa and rejected the culture that was closest to Africa, which would be blues, gospel, and Negro spirituals. I doubt if I was ever considered an exponent of the Black Arts Movement in literature. If I was, I am not aware of it.

Antonucci: The reason I ask is when I was looking back at *Half Black Half Blacker* (1970), I was surprised. It was not the entry point that I expected. Maybe it would help if you spoke about working with Third World Press and OBAC as an emerging artist in the 1970s. What did you learn during this period as a poet, an educator, and an artist?

Plumpp: What I found was that if you are an artist or cultural worker, you have to seize the moment and every opportunity to shape your vision as a writer and hone your craft. OBAC was a great movement in that it gathered voices of diversity and some merit and created this incredible local dialogue among the writers. But then again, it was a dangerous movement when you begin to speak of something that was revolutionary: Martin Luther King was not revolutionary; Malcolm X did not propose anything revolutionary. Neither proposed the overthrow and exchange of this government with a socialist government.

The unwritten agenda of black arts and the black aesthetic was how to empower African Americans in publishing, criticism, and scholarship. That's what it concretely led to. Therefore, you would get Amiri Baraka who would write "Black Literature," but whose aesthetic was definitely Beat, whose black aesthetic was amorphous at the level of the printed page. So you are not having Baraka talk about the literary craft of *Preface to a Twenty Volume Suicide Note* or *The Dead Lecturer* and how his blues/jazz sensibility reforms or articulates aspects of the Beat aesthetic. In early works I get this incredible poet and then I come to get this performer and often reproductions of his performances.

This kind of literature appealed to the masses and exhorted people to rise up and claim their blackness, to rise up and excoriate the white demons, to rise up and reach out to touch Mother Africa. They became canonic and Baraka became the leading black aesthetic poet to some. I thought that person was Larry Neal because of his ability to write about jazz and his ability to locate and individualize its iconography in his poems. Without a doubt. There's no doubt about that.

Still, working with Third World Press offered me a way of meeting my public both vertically and horizontally. It helped me get known, get anthologized. I could get a job at the university.

Other Third World people could see my work and help me to progress. It made the potential Sterling Plumpp into a published writer and I am indebted.

Antonucci: Would you, then, let people call you an example of the Black Arts Movement legacy?

Plumpp: No, as long as people understand that—to borrow from Leon Forrest—the Black Arts Movement was as angular as any other movement; I was not a Black Arts poet poured from some mold. I was attempting to create one for myself.

Antonucci: If I can keep you in this moment, in *Black Rituals* you write: "Don L. Lee is really an old-time preacher using street symbols, corner raps, and the Black Position as his bibles. . . . The problem the Black man faces today is for Don L. Lee to get a church and carry on the tradition of a Bishop Turner" (99). I wonder if you see this church in today's black cultural landscape?

Plumpp: Yes, I think that Don L. Lee did find his church; I think his church is a combination of Third World Press and the New Concept School. Because what Haki did with the fortune that he made through speaking and teaching and publishing is that he poured it all back into Third World Press, purchased state of the art property to direct it, gave jobs to the black community, and founded a school. There is no doubt that he is a very important institution builder whose specialty is publishing and educating.

Antonucci: And you were a witness to this process: I mean you participated in bringing . . .

Plumpp: I was the first director of the Institute for Positive Education; I was an editor at Third World Press; I was the first managing editor of *Black Books Bulletin.*

Antonucci: As well as somebody setting up a black studies/African American studies program at a university in Chicago. Would you comment on this part of the institution building process?

Plumpp: The institutionalization of African American studies allowed African Americans to garner a space from which they could gain the resources to insure a number of things: First, and most important, literary texts, scholarly texts, and research concerning black subjects would be taught permanently here at the University of Illinois–Chicago. Number two, the students here at UIC would have a viable alternative to other majors and avenues for education; and finally, it would be a space from which to advocate for African Americans and more Americans of diverse backgrounds.

Antonucci: This is something that you get to in *Black Rituals.* You use an interesting term when you talk about the period between 1967 and 1970 as the "intermediary period." This is the period when black studies programs were . . .

Plumpp: Becoming institutionalized. I mean you have to remember that many of the founding figures of African American studies were people who had to retool their academic specialty on the battlefield. They had not really studied African American literary texts while they were in graduate school. They were not allowed to. Many really had not studied African Americans as research subjects; they had gone about laying the groundwork by working in a non-African American context. By l978 you start to get the emergence of top African American graduate students from UCLA, Yale, or Harvard, who mastered the literary canon and its concomitant theory so that they could speak in one voice about African American literature and the literature of the world as well. The same impulse was happening in other disciplines, such as sociology. What this did was transform the standard of African American studies and the immediate impact of this was that these people became very competitive and qualified to teach at the top schools and you get this transformation or even consolidation of the field.

Antonucci: This isn't what you anticipated back in 1968 . . .

Plumpp: I had no idea what would happen—I mean, I thought that major texts and major studies of African American life and culture should be studied seriously at different levels. What was happening was that the political democratization of America was being followed by a democratization of its education system and the result was that this country had to begin looking at its own diversity.

Antonucci: Would you care to comment on the emergence of a transnational diasporic consciousness or identities within African American/Africana studies?

Plumpp: This is very complex. The decolonization of the African continent is a difficult concept to grasp, as if the enormity of the trans-Atlantic slave trade, which went on between 1533 and 1803 legally and went on in reality until decolonization in 1975. I mean the danger is this: If people are speaking about some monolithic Africa which has yet to be defined by the boundaries and domains of research, then I think this can become very, very dangerous. But if one is looking at how Africans use their culture and their wit to confront temporary realities in real African societies, then it can be a positive thing because it forces African Americans to see the trans-Atlantic slave trade as a way for providing labor for those who were colonizing the New World. If it takes some kinds of narrow Afrocentrism to make these kinds of distinctions, then I am going to ask "Afrocentric from where?" I mean, is it a Zulu worldview, a Hausa worldview, a Yoruba worldview? A generic Afrocentrism cannot be tied to geography or culture.

Those who attempt to undertake this project should be lauded, but when I was in South Africa, I found a whole lot of young black people who were Marxists. I came to realize that they were not Marxists because they were mixed up or wanted an assimilation with white people. They had become Marxists because they wanted bread, a job, and somewhere to lie down. There simply was nobody else other than the Communist Party, who was as forcefully in these areas as the Marxists were.

Antonucci: You became involved in the South African liberation/anti-apartheid movement in the 1980s. One early product of this work was the *Somehow We Survive* anthology of South African poetry. What drew you to the writing that came out of this struggle?

Plumpp: Several things. My closest friend was a South African attached to the ANC (African National Congress), Keorapetse Kgositsile. I had known him since 1972. I had known Dennis Brutus from about the same time, and

I had known Mongane Serote. What this means is that I had the names of the people who were being detained and murdered on file as well as all of the literary works that were being written and published under these circumstances. I suppose that in some ways there is a similarity between the struggle in South Africa and the continuing struggle that African Americans have in this country to organize themselves politically to get certain kinds of resources. Finally, the music that was composed in the South African cities—the work of Hugh Masekela, Dorothy Masuka, and Miriam Makeba—that music reminded me of jazz and Negro spirituals.

Antonucci: You mention Kgositsile. He is central to the volume's production. Can you talk more about your relationship with this South African poet and his work?
Plumpp: First of all he is extremely well educated, erudite, and grounded in political theory. At the same time, he is a great lover of blues and jazz. This is really where our connection begins. We are somehow connected by the music. He was instrumental to *Somehow We Survive* when I was seeking material for the volume. He helped me get work from ANC writers who were underground at the time.

Antonucci: In the volume you also give credit to Michael Anania for pushing you toward undertaking this project . . .
Plumpp: Michael supported me in a number of levels through the tenure process and the promotion to full professor. He is knowledgeable about the publishing world and when the opportunity to work on *Somehow We Survive* came, he gave me pointers and was able to talk about this literature in the same way that he was able to talk about African American literature. I was encouraged by what he said.

Antonucci: Have you continued to keep up with South African poetry since the fall of the Pretoria government and would you consider editing a companion volume to *Somehow We Survive* featuring more recent works by poets of South Africa?
Plumpp: I keep in contact with Keorapetse. You see, a great deal of South African literature that was being published [in the 1970s and 1980s] was underwritten by funds from outside of the country. Now, finally, there is something of a publishing system being developed from within. I would not have undertaken this project if Black South Africans had not allowed me to do it. Now, I would like to work with a South African poet as a consulting

editor on a project that tried to get a grip on the complexity of South African literature from Zulu to Kosa to work written in Afrikaans. I mean to really look at the whole body of work written by these Africans over a long period of time. I do think that a group of South African editors would be best suited to do this, but I would play any part that I could to develop a project and do that.

Antonucci: Are there any lasting images or impressions of South Africa under apartheid that have stayed with you? I'm thinking about your work in *Johannesburg and Other Poems*; you touch on the connections between life in the United States and under the Pretoria regime in poems like "L.A. Riot" and "Logged in My Eyes."

Plumpp: There was an incurable optimism when I was in South Africa. People knew that things were going to change and things were going to change for the good. I suppose that my image of South Africa is that it was a nation with millions of children who had a sense that the world would change because of their doing.

There is a line by a poet from Guyana named Martin Carter. I forget the name of the poem, but the first line is: "I rise from the nigger yards of the world." He didn't say black: Whatever peonage did for me as a black peasant in Mississippi, the cruelty of the mining industry did to the black people there in South Africa.

Antonucci: This might be a good point to begin a discussion of *Blues Narratives*. This is your account of two lives grown deep in the black cultural practices of Mississippi. After reading the poems in preparation for today, I selected a set of lines and phrases taken from the poem to your grandfather Victor that present "the blues as. . . ." I hoped that you might respond or fill in the blank when I say, for example, "the blues as a tight song."

Plumpp: Well, yeah. I think that coming, as it did in the postbellum period, with the coming of a reactionary regime and the racial politics of the South which turned back the clock and erased the thirteenth, fourteenth, and fifteenth amendment protection for African Americans and instituted the Black Codes, for someone to stand up and sing about his black life, to see that life as being important enough to sing about, is a supreme act of defiance. My grandfather would have been about sixteen years old when blues appeared in about 1895. So through hindsight, not that I saw my grandfather as a blues singer when I was coming up, as I wrote more and more, I began to see my grandfather as an embodiment of this blues figure.

Antonucci: "Blues as remediation . . ."
Plumpp: In this sense: Coming up in this society with the history of chattel slavery on one's back leaves a person destined to fall victim to the deadly disease of what W. E. B. DuBois called "double consciousness." To the extent that one has double consciousness, one has great difficulties crafting a vision or plan for one's self and in fact blues is a remediation course to accelerate those individuals' ability to learn how to have their own personal vision and not see the world through the eyes of those who would "look down on them with amused contempt and pity." This way the blues is a crash course in reality.

Antonucci: "The blues as a naming license . . ."
Plumpp: Yeah—I mean what happens to you if you're an American; your self worth is so pulverized that one dare not name oneself. But within the blues, one can call oneself "Mr. Pitiful" or "The Tail Dragger." The ability to name, and the ritual of the blues gives one a license to name. I think the preacher has this license to name too.

Antonucci: "Blues as home . . ."
Plumpp: This is not so much in the physical sense and not so much for African Americans alone. But I am thinking more of those who can gain epiphany into the experience. Blues opens a door that says "Welcome. I am glad to see you prodigal son or prodigal daughter. Welcome." Then, it embraces you.

Antonucci: If you will, let me read from Canto Five:

> When the mid
> wife carved me from
> your fate
> bound my reaches
> for your mother
>
> and I can remember
> no cries
> for your absences.

This is a blues, correct?
Plumpp: Yes.

Antonucci: If I were to take this down to several critics, some would say, "No, this is not blues. It does not have AAB rhyme pattern. It does not show any of the standard blues signature." How then is this blues?
Plumpp: I guess this is blues in the Ellisonian sense. Willie Dixon said that blues is the facts of life. For Willie Dixon, blues is nothing but a good man feeling bad. I think Ellison said that the blues is the impulse to keep the painful details of a brutal experience alive in one's aching consciousness and to overcome them, not by the consolation of a philosophy, but by fingering the jagged grain in its tragic and comic lyricism; in that sense, it is a blues. I think that Ellison also said that Louis Armstrong made art out of his invisibility.

Antonucci: To step back quickly to something that was not being acknowledged during the Black Arts moment . . .
Plumpp: I think that Armstrong would have been looked at as a clown at that time because of his smile without understanding the content of the man's character and the content of the man's music. He was a true genius. It's not clear that he was doing what he was doing for the benefit of his white benefactors or whether he was doing this for their detriment.

Antonucci: This is another question that comes directly from lines in the Victor Emmanuel section of *Blues Narratives*. "History is not a river. . . . If not this, then what is history?" So much of this poem and the blues are about history, the past and lived experience.
Plumpp: I think, somewhere, I've said that history is an island that one drags as one negotiates one's way through life. I like to think of history as an island in bountiful waters that we fish from. You see, with history you don't go anywhere, physically. It's like when Charlie Parker and Dizzy Gillespie came into African American music, they carried with them a certain history that gave them certain improvisational ways of playing which allowed them to go where they wanted to go.

The primary difference between a Charlie Parker and a black peasant, who shared much of the same history, is that Parker had the space to use his imagination. I say Parker because not everybody that blows a horn was able to do what he did with that space. Blues creates the space where history resides. And with certain insights into the history within that space, the potential for one to grow becomes almost infinite.

Antonucci: Two last questions: let's use the blues to move into the first section of *Blues Narratives*: The way that blues alternate with the narrative in the first section creates the space for the voice(s) to come out. Is this in a literary sense an example of the blues making this space for expression?

Plumpp: Yes. Several things: it dawns on me that the persona of the poet's son could never exist without the space created by the blues singer mother. That's why it took that form. For fifteen or twenty years, I could not write about my mother. I didn't do that until I saw that she was really a blues singer.

Antonucci: So, and please don't count this question against me, what's going on in that first section is a call and response; what is unclear is who is calling and who is responding.

Plumpp: What is clear is that the sections begin and end with the blues. What also is clear is that the standard English poet narrator does not have the keys to the door of imagination. Somehow the larger blues experience is not only articulating a part of him that is in memory but is also teaching him the task of how to become someone who can articulate or narrate his own story. That's why the dialogue is taking place.

Antonucci: "Every step I take is quick sand . . ." Because this is a very serious business.

Plumpp: It is so serious that the female/mother persona would have to be either a bitch or a whore, a girl or an Annie, someone fucked and fucked over, someone completely dehumanized then discarded. I mean, in trying to look at the totality of that situation, that part of the task of the poet in writing is to use naturalistic blues language to describe or articulate that dilemma.

Antonucci: It is successful, very successful. The last question is one we've talked about in other conversations: Could you speak to the relationship between blues and jazz?

Plumpp: I suppose that in a very simple way, jazz to me ain't nothing but blues with a little education. And if I had been born in 1876 and matriculated at an all-black college and tried to articulate myself and the black experience in music or song, I might have come up doing jazz. But if I had been born in the same year on a plantation in the Mississippi Delta without that kind of exposure, I might have been a big brother to Robert Johnson. Having said that, there is invention and improvisation in both traditions, but here is the difference: Blues singers tend to work with a stock set of songs that one generation rewrites without claiming authorship. To put it another way, the cliché of one generation is revised and renamed and recommissioned by a blues singer. In jazz, it appears to me that virtuosity is a given and what the jazz musician literally does is cartograph the geography of the instrument being played.

The blues singer is a brilliant creative artist who might have an idea of entertainment because he knows the tradition. The jazz musician is not necessarily an entertainer because he knows the tradition. He knows that his task is to create music in the landscape of his imagination. So the jazz musician is constantly giving God's great earth more space, while the blues singer creates a space out of that space. I think that they are both a celebration and affirmation, but I find more individuality in blues. I find more variation with the blues in that you have a folk form that will not perform the same function of someone who has mastered the folk form and created an imaginative, personalized form like jazz.

Antonucci: And you bring this home through your poetry. Thank you.
Plumpp: Thank you.

Sterling Plumpp: Interview

Reginald Gibbons / 2003

From *TriQuarterly* (April 27, 2010). Reprinted by permission of the author.

This interview was recorded on three afternoons in September and October of 2003. A small portion of it was published in *Arkansas Review: A Journal of Delta Studies*, in 2005. This is the first publication of the full text.

Sterling Plumpp and I met in the lounge of the Arts Club of Chicago, recorded for an hour or more, and then continued our discussions over lunch, where I took a few additional notes on his comments and added these to the transcript. I edited the full version by putting together Plumpp's separate comments about one subject or another to form four sections, each with a focus.

Plumpp retired from his professorship at the University of Illinois at Chicago at the end of 2001—a tall, physically powerful-looking man in his early sixties, an intellectually powerful man who is also an energetic talker. His conversation reveals his interest in both the literary and the political. Many are the boundaries across which his experience has taken him: familial, social, linguistic, educational, literary and artistic, musical, political, geographical. This interview can encompass only a little of what Plumpp has to say, and I would especially like to hear more of his observations on the Mississippi of his birth and youth, and the Chicago of his young manhood. I hope there will be other occasions for him to convey some of his extraordinary and extraordinarily representative personal journey to readers.

There was lots of laughter from Sterling Plumpp during these hours of interviewing—laughter that cannot be transcribed, although once in a great while, where it is particularly expressive, I have indicated it in brackets. I would call this laughter the mark of intellectual glee, which does not mean happiness. I think that Plumpp was laughing simply because of his pleasure in thinking about poetry, history, and African America, and because the history he knows so well (social, political, and literary) is so fraught with dilemmas, contradictions, and nearly incomprehensible outcomes. One can laugh not only with triumph or irony, astonishment or puzzlement, but with admiration for wit and courage and endurance, and also with dismay and sheer wonder at sorrow, weakness, defeat, and injustice.

That Plumpp's work is substantially represented in Keith Gilyard's recent anthology of African American writing (2004); is the subject of an essay by John Edgar Wideman; and has been the focus of two small literary magazines, *Arkansas Review* and *Valley Voices*, may mean that this poet, so independent and original, has begun to receive a portion of his due recognition. His unique fusion of a rhythmic fragmentation of language and flowing song is an artistic accomplishment of the first rank, an achievement with the degree of originality, emotional intensity, and intellectual power that we regard as great. In addition—it is needless to say, but would be an omission not to say—Plumpp's poetic mode is analogous to the virtuosity of a master of post-bebop. Poetry, though, however rich its language may be in sound and rhythm, is unlike music in that it says what it means while it is singing. The meanings and the materials in Plumpp's poetry—narratives of defeat and triumph, of lives most often excluded from public discourse, forgotten circumstances of humble life, metaphors drawn from field work and house work and hard work of all kinds, repetitions drawn from the blues, syntax repeatedly constructed to be expressive of multifarious signifying—are among the most necessary in American poetry.

Background

Sterling Plumpp: My aunt was on her deathbed with a stroke. She's my mother's sister, so I would go take care of her. She had a second-floor tenant who had the most powerful metaphor for black people I've seen, although he used the stereotype. He said, "Yestiddy evening," he said, "niggahs out here on the porch like blackbirds on fences." And the interesting thing about the metaphor is that when blackbirds are on the fences, they are almost like they are in battle formation; they're not timid anymore, they own the turf. There's something about the body language of the blackbird on the fence that you can reach out and touch. And it couldn't be one blackbird—they're in numbers. There's something healthy about that image which led me to see a great deal of validity in what sociologists and newspapers call the ghetto. It's not negative at all. There's something about ownership of that place and that space, that language, the way they walk—they sell drugs there because they own that land. There's something about that that I find healthy. It's destructive, but there's something about that attitude that says, "Hell no, these people ain't going to die no time soon."

Reginald Gibbons: A figure of strength.
SP: Yeah. It's almost like the elation I felt when I saw *New Jack City*. I don't like drug dealers, but there's something about the emergence of Nino Brown, this African American who says, "This might be hell but shit I'm gonna rule it. I'm runnin' this. Ain't nobody gonna come in here and do anything except obey the laws that I construct. This is a business and I run it."

RG: A capitalist business.
SP: But I run it. In this very decadent kind of place you get this kind of Toussaint L'Ouverture figure who's defining turf independence. That's what this is about.

RG: And defying the colonial power? Leon Forrest used to refer to the so-called ghettos as "occupied zones."
SP: But this blood has defined a sphere of independence that's independent. It's an independent zone. I love it.

RG: Would you mind saying something about your family, and about Sanders Bottom?
SP: My maternal grandparents reared me from a time before I can remember until I was about fifteen years old. My grandfather died when I was fourteen years old, and I lived with my grandmother an additional two years. My grandfather was born in 1880, in Hinds County [Mississippi]—that's the county where the state capital, Jackson, is—and he died in 1955.

Two salient points about his maturation: one is that when he was fourteen years old, he was in school, and someone threw a spitball and hit the teacher. She turned to him and asked him who did it, and he said he didn't know. She was going to whip him and make him tell her. She brought a switch down and it hit him on the ear. And he lifted her up and took her to the heater—a wood-burning heater—in an attempt to burn her up, and his brothers and sisters stopped him.

The teacher's name was Mrs. Mahoney—at that time I think there must have been white teachers. She told his mother that if she herself would come to school and whip Victor, he could come back to school, or if his mother would allow her, the teacher, to whip him, he could come back to school.

His mother told him that now he was a man, and he did not go back. He was in the fourth grade, this child. About fourteen years old—I don't know.

The other story is that there had been a horse that was very difficult to ride, and that one day while his mother was at church he went out and tried to ride the horse. The horse threw him, and this broke his shoulder. The story was that he had been so tough that he never told her about it, and for the remainder of his life, his left shoulder was higher than his right shoulder. Was permanently distorted. That's by way of background.

My grandmother was born in 1890, and she died in 1993 at the age of 103. She also had two sisters who lived to be 100. The story that she told me, all her life, is that her mother had two children—herself and a brother a couple of years younger, by the name of Riley. Outside of wedlock. Then she was marrying a man who was very light, and he said that he wanted her, but he didn't want those little nigger children. So her parents, the children's grand-parents, took them to school, and after church one day, asked would any-body take these children, because their mother couldn't take care of them, wouldn't take care of them. And her father's sister took her in—and made her a servant, in her estimation.

Her brother Riley was so recalcitrant that he was given away to a white man to take care of, and the white man said that Riley had left, and it was not known whether he had left or he was killed, and his body never discovered.

So she lived with the Leamuses, doing all the work. Then when she became a woman, her cousin made sexual advances toward her, and when she told her uncle, he said he didn't care what happened to her since there was no blood between them, only marriage. Her aunt took her back to her mother, and since her mother was happily married, she couldn't live there, so [her mother] took [her] to church to find her a husband.

RG: How old was she then?

SP: She would have been about twenty-one or twenty-two. She was married at about twenty-three. She was born in 1890; she got married in 1913. And that way she found my grandfather, who came to church but who at that time had just got religion. He had been a gambler, someone who drank alcohol. And they were married for the next forty years or so, until he died. They had seven children, born between 1914 and 1929.

RG: And one of those was your mother?

SP: One was my mother. There was one born in 1914, one born in 1916, my mother born in 1920, an aunt born in 1922, an uncle born in 1924, an aunt born in 1925, and an uncle born in 1929. And now all of them are deceased. They died between 1980 and 2001.

RG: They did not all have the longevity of those hundred-year-olds?
SP: One lived to be eighty-seven. And one lived to be eighty-one . . . And as I understand it, Sanders Bottom was what would have been known as "heir property."

RG: What does that mean?
SP: It would have been land that the family would have gotten somehow after slavery. You would be entitled to it if you were part of the family. But you wouldn't have a deed to it. You could go there and build a house or be buried. This was called "heir property." My grandfather never wanted anything to do with it, because of the way my grandmother had been treated when she was a child—but this is my grandmother's testimony. But it was her testimony when she was in her fifties, and it was her testimony when I talked to her when she was in her late nineties. It was either true, or she believed it to be true. But for me, Sanders Bottom becomes a metaphor for the legacy of slavery in terms of my family relationship to the land: a difficult place to work, a difficult place to make a living. And outside of that land, you had the structure of segregation, of Jim Crow, intimidating and dehumanizing.

RG: And your mother?
SP: It's complex. In 1937, the day after she turned seventeen, my mother gave birth to my brother, the first child she had outside of wedlock. She was living with my grandfather and grandmother. In 1940, I was the second child born, about eight months before she became twenty, but in 1941, she married a GI and moved away to Louisiana, and I don't have any recollection of her until my sister was born in 1944. So I never bonded with her. She was not my mother—she was not the mother *present*; she was not the mother figure. She was my biological mother, but I have absolutely no recollection of her as my mother until I am four years old, when I am told that she is my mother. None. It's not there.

RG: A lot of people can't remember anything from before that age.
SP: No, no—she was *not there*, Reginald! But then I know that she *is* my mother. But then I don't live with her at all until I'm about seventeen years old.

RG: She became a dominant figure in your imagination in the creation of your *Blues Narratives*, along with your grandfather.

SP: She *is* the reason that I'm here. And there's nothing I can do about my childhood, the first sixteen or seventeen years of my life. She was not blessed with longevity so I could sit and talk to her about this complex kind of relationship I suppose she and I had. But I also knew that I couldn't go forward without dealing with that part of the puzzle of my existence. I tried to deal with it when she died in 1980. And I couldn't. And it's only somewhere between 1995 and 2000 that I developed a kind of formula of how I could deal with the fact that I had been born a peasant and somehow been educated, and she had been born a peasant and her imagination seemed to remain within the orbit of folk dictates. So I don't feel disappointment—is that the word? Because I simply wasn't there. She didn't do anything bad; I wasn't there. Maybe I was hurt by the circumstances of her death; cancer killed her on the installment plan.

RG: How old was she when she died?

SP: She was fifty-nine.

RG: And how did you get your education?

SP: I suppose the earliest recollection that I have had about education was the story of Booker T. Washington. How he had been a slave. How he had been a fully grown man who could neither read nor write when slavery ended. How he worked hard all day and stayed up all night with the light of a candle, learning to read. Then how he goes on, a year after he graduates from Hampton Institute, and founds Tuskegee Institute. Then maybe I remember hearing about George Washington Carver, who arose from humble origin to become the Nobel-level candidate in biology with what he did with the peanut. I knew that literacy was an invaluable tool in one's quest for both self-definition and self-empowerment. So I always wanted to be educated.

However, due to the situation I found myself in, I didn't go to school at all until I was eight years old. I went to school initially in the fall of 1948, which would have put me almost three years behind. And never went to school a full term. I never went to school when school opened, and I was never at school when school ended. After the cotton had been picked, and all that stuff, I went to school; and when you started working the land, I quit. Therefore, in 1955, right before I turned fifteen, I moved to Jackson, and I'm in seventh grade. I go to a Catholic school and begin to do pretty well.

I made B's. But it's only in high school that I made the straight A. I read the book. I read the textbook, to figure out how to answer the questions. Didn't have a lot of books, but I read them. And studied. And then won a tuition-paid scholarship to Saint Benedict's College in Atchison, Kansas, and it was there that I was exposed to Western literature. Because at that time, forty-three years ago, everybody had to take Western Civilization and Western Literature.

You began with the Greeks, with the *Iliad*, with the *Odyssey*, and then you came down through the plays—Aeschylus and Euripides—then the *Divine Comedy*. Not just *Inferno* but the whole *Divine Comedy* and some of the lesser works by Dante. *Don Quixote.* Milton: *Paradise Lost* as well as lesser work—"Samson Agonistes." It inflamed the imagination. In the words of Richard Wright, I suppose, it excites an unquenchable hunger.

By the second year, I read "Sonny's Blues" by James Baldwin. And a funny thing happened in my mind. I had known when I read Dante, because of the way he was able to position people in this created world where he wanted them, putting popes and kings in hell—I knew the power of literature. There was no doubt about that. And I also knew the difficulty of faith, because I couldn't understand why God would do what they did to Prometheus. You know—I'm a good Catholic boy, I didn't understand, I didn't get it. But at the same time, what Aeschylus was doing as a writer made me say, Oh yeah. These poets had been at work when I had ridden the back seats of buses in Mississippi.

No one told me the power of mythology—I discovered mythology through the written word. And if this is true (although I did not come to that conclusion, maybe I began that quest), perhaps what they are telling me about the god who formed this universe and his angels, perhaps that's a mythology, too! Perhaps that's a mythology that I can unravel. And in unraveling that mythology, maybe some of the things haunting my superego would dissipate.

RG: That's a lot to happen to a young man in college! You published early books in Detroit. Did you go from college to there?
SP: No, I came from college to Chicago, and I was looking for a job, because my aunt could not support me any longer as a student, and I was looking for a job to make some money.

RG: She was here in Chicago?
SP: She was in Mississippi.

I got a job at the Chicago post office. Now, here are all these ideas, and I was working seven days a week, ten hours a day, and I still enrolled at Roosevelt University to take classes (I had been in college for two years at Saint Benedict). A fascinating thing happened: you confront that cold world of the city. People bleeding, being hit upside the head—but people partying. I was in my youth and didn't understand it. We got paid every two weeks, and some people, if they got paid this Friday they wouldn't have any money next Friday, or they would go out and engage in sexual escapades that they had to talk about . . .

Understanding up close what it means to be human. And at the time, reading everything James Baldwin had written, everything Richard Wright had written. Langston Hughes, Ralph Ellison, I read all of it. I discovered Amiri Baraka, everything DuBois had written.

And you compartmentalize—oppression will do that to you: black people didn't have any of the upper-echelon jobs; the job at the post office was considered a "good government job." I'm twenty-two years old, supposed to be glad to be there, perhaps for the next thirty years, and I said, Hell no—no, I'm going to write books.

Now, people there said that everybody who came through the door was going to write books—about all sorts of naked humanity: people being thrown down stairs because they got some money from a juice man and didn't pay it back; in many instances a white supervisor was caught in sexual intercourse with black women and the black women getting suspended or fired. You name it, it was happening.

I became politically active. I would picket before I would come to work. And then—bam!—at the end of '63 I had to go into the army, for two years. It's the worst thing that happened to me, and it's probably the best thing that happened to me. Because unlike the post office where I was working those ten hours a day, seven days a week, I was in with these young men who did young-man things, and I was black and bookish, and I wanted to be a writer.

In fact, one of the first things I did, in early 1964, I found out that Baldwin's *Blues for Mister Charlie* was playing at the ANTA Theater in New York. I took a bus to New York, got off the bus in New York, took a train to my aunt's house—she was living in Queens—took the train to Harlem . . . I can remember asking people, "Do you know how to get to the ANTA Theater?" and they said no, and I said, "Do you know where it is?" and they said no, but it didn't take me long to figure that if I go away from Harlem and I get off in Grand Central Station or somewhere down there, it was easy. So I found the ANTA Theater there, and I also saw Baldwin, saw Diana Sands and Al Freeman, Jr. in the play. Which was brilliantly acted. Jim Cunningham sent me Ellison's *Shadow and Act* [1964], sent me Baraka's *Dutchman* [1964], while I was in the army. I continued to try to write.

Before you have ever written anything, there's a mystery of how you do what Jayne Cortez calls, "put your mouth on paper." You don't know exactly what the science of that is. So although I wrote a lot of autobiography—I was just jotting things down. The civil rights movement was going bad, people were being killed . . . A terrible time. All these things happening in Africa— Lumumba killed back in 1961; Kenya; and the war is heating up in Vietnam. But then you're twenty-four, twenty-five, trying to write, you don't know . . .

So I came out of the army with about two thousand dollars' worth of records, because I listened to records all day, and the music that I liked best, probably in terms of my soul, maybe wasn't blues, but folk music. Odetta. Maybe I still have about twenty LPs of Odetta. I loved the stories—I loved the narratives of these plain people who often have to do heroic deeds. I had seen blues in person. Then I learned jazz—I listened to Coltrane and Charlie Parker in the army.

It's confusing. When you are rural, and you go see blues, and you're educated, people think that that's your entire life. So when I say that I went to see Howlin' Wolf at Sylvio's on the West Side, I also went down to McKie's to see Kenny Dorham, to the Plug Nickel to see Thelonius Monk, somewhere to see Little Esther, Stanley Turrentine, Sonny Stitt. But I also went to the Regal to see the Five Du-Tones, Little Stevie Wonder, Rufus Thomas, Freddy King.

In other words, I think that that is very confusing to whites who become aficionados of blues. They don't know the difference between a juke joint and a show club. And much of the blues in the black community was in juke joints. Show clubs, they would have shake dancers, and you would get dressed up and go. But see, if you are educated you get access—so if you interview anyone my age who is black and educated, they had access to *all* that. But if they were simply a worker they would not have had access to the jazz.

RG: Did you move to New York?
SP: No, I visited my aunt. I went to New York specifically to see *Blues for Mister Charlie*.

RG: At Saint Benedict, had someone actually assigned "Sonny's Blues" as reading?

SP: No, it must have been in a book edited by Herbert Gold, I want to think, as part of Western Literature—after John Dos Passos and Faulkner, we came to the contemporary and to Baldwin, and "Sonny's Blues" was the story in the book. The professor, maybe it was Professor Newman, not a monk but a layperson, who told me that Baldwin was a black writer. Then I read the black encyclopedia. I read everything I could get on James Baldwin. I even read *Giovanni's Room* [1956; a paperback was issued in 1966]. By the time *The Fire Next Time* [1963] came, I had read everything he had written, before. Then I'm at a different point in my life—*Another Country* [1962; paperback 1968], *The Fire Next Time*—and when I read those books I feel let down. Maybe except for *Going to Meet the Man* [1965; paperback 1967], which is a collection of short stories. But that was the drama, the life I was seeing every day. To make art out of that! And I suppose I was intrigued by the black and white world that I found in *Another Country*. The understanding was not between people who were intellectuals; they were artists, outlaw types, outcasts, maybe. In the post office, I had been told that if I read so much of Baldwin, I might be switching, too!

RG: And your connection with Haki Madhubuti when he was Don L. Lee?
SP: After I got out of the army, I still wanted to be a writer. I would write, but then I had to get a degree, so I went to Roosevelt University and got a degree in psychology in 1968. And around 1966 or 1967, I met Don selling *Think Black* [1970], and I bought copies, got his phone number, and eventually did *Black Pride*. I gave him some poems and eventually they were published. When they first founded the OBAC Writers Workshops and began to talk about black writing and the black aesthetic, I was fascinated by that, but a lot of what they were saying was not jibing with the writer I loved, James Baldwin. I knew Baldwin's critique of Richard Wright and protest literature. I knew Ellison's critique. And I never thought that I had read anyone who knew more about black culture than Ralph Ellison. I don't know what I thought about Ellison's need to create all of these white literary godfathers, or something like that—I don't know that they ever created any *godsons* that looked like him!

But it doesn't make any difference whether it's Faulkner or whoever—you learn from whoever you learn from. And obviously there are a lot of great writers. So a lot of Ellison's policy-implication sort of statements disturbed me, but I thought that he was a genius as a writer. Unmatched, in one novel. Very few people in the twentieth century match him in one book. And among those who do match him could very well be Faulkner and

Leon Forrest. I think that Forrest's *Divine Days* might, in time. But then, I'm southern. . . .

This idea of being a revolutionary writer—black power, black conscious-ness, at the individual level, is incredibly important. But if you look at some of the issues that were raised about Richard Wright by both Baldwin and Ellison, one of the things that you find yourself doing is putting yourself in a box where literature has to be didactic; you're simplifying it, and you can't get out of that box, on the one hand. On the other hand, you say that your model for literature is in jazz, but you don't see any work that's being pub-lished that has any of the complexity of jazz.

One of the things, it seems to me, that Broadside Press was exploiting, was what they thought was the new black vernacular, street language—and not the language maybe of Jay Wright. You see? Where is the complexity? Some people even attacked Robert Hayden. I love Brooks, but she never had the mastery of black history that that man had. "Runagate, Runagate," "Middle Passage"!

You can't intimidate people into falling in line with your popular ideo-logical kind of statement. And just because people disagree with your state-ment doesn't necessarily mean that they betray black people. I thought that was a real tragedy. The other tragedy was that Amiri Baraka, whose writing I love—the idea that he needs to give up his white wife and come to Harlem. I don't think I need him to do that, and I don't think Harlem needed him to do that. They need you to be honest, LeRoi. And it does not appear that he took the same care with writing and constructing his poems after he moved uptown, that he was doing downtown. That's the only observation I want to make. It seemed to me that he was informed more by the aesthetics of jazz, at the level of writing, when he was downtown.

RG: You have said about Brooks that her virtuosity is part of her commentary.

SP: I do feel that for all the people who talk about Brooks and her blackness, Brooks and her "relevance," Brooks and perhaps that *Maud Martha* was written for white folks—I think they miss the point; they miss the whole damn point of what she was doing as a poet. The fact that she had mas-tered the ballad form, and the mock epic or whatever you want to call *Annie Allen*, the fact that she had put so much virtuosity and mastery in that book, elevates the theme that she is writing about. That's what that does. That's what that does.

RG: Did you want to write fiction, after reading Baldwin?

SP: I wanted to write fiction all my life, so I could get away from what James Baldwin calls the difficult task of keeping body and soul together by working! I still think I can tell stories, but the poetry came. My preoccupation with language, getting all wrapped up in language—here I am with my gift from God to write poetry, and I'm complaining about something, and this [once] made Leon Forrest tell me that I better be damn glad I could write anything!

RG: But you went from the desire to write fiction to the accomplishment of writing poetry. And you wrote early prose books. Did Don Lee publish your first book of poems?

SP: Don Lee published *Portable Soul* [1969], *Half Black Half Blacker* [1970], and *Steps to Break the Circle* [1974].

RG: How did that feel to you, when your first book came out?

SP: I suppose that what you imagine in typescript is always magical when you see it in print. Although it was not that elegant, and the book sort of seeped away. And Broadside published *Clinton* [1976]. It marked a very important change in my life, because Thunder's Mouth Press then published *Somehow We Survive* [1982] and *The Mojo Hands Call, I Must Go.* Everything else had been a chapbook, but *The Mojo Hands Call, I Must Go* won the Carl Sandburg Literary Prize. It was published in 1982 and won the prize in 1983. And then, the next two books are published by Another Chicago Press—because Lee Webster had been the editor at Thunder's Mouth, and they split up. And the books that really sold more were *Blues: The Story Always Untold* [1989] and then *Johannesburg and Other Poems* [1993].

And by that time, the major concerns that I am involved with—identity, history, the South, blues, social change, South Africa—have been dealt with, and maybe the next three books, that form a coherent whole, are the next project, which is more being a self-conscious poet trying to deal with language and legacy, and that would be *Horn Man* [1996], *Ornate with Smoke* [1997], and *Velvet BeBop Kente Cloth* [2003]. Because what I'm trying to deal with there is the fact that I'm simply not a blues singer—and just as educated African Americans had to confront their folk past with the technique of jazz, somehow I had to bring the technique of jazz to my blues poetry in order to develop a personal voice. And by the time that I got to *Ornate with Smoke*, I was hearing language—I had been hearing it all along, and I didn't know what to do with what I was hearing. And at some point I felt that I had to follow where the language led. And that led to *Ornate with Smoke*.

Bebop led me into *Horn Man*—I'm looking at a bebopper—and that led me to watch him specifically as that. What I found in *Ornate with Smoke* [is that] I would be looking at the post-bop beboppers, and some of their devices. And by the time I got to *Velvet BeBop Kente Cloth*, I had allowed this post-bop bebopper to become a narrator and comment on the importance of bebop. Because bebop becomes the moment when people find their voices in some kind of collective process of innovation.

Now, *Blues Narratives* is entirely different, because it grows out of this need—if I were to make the statement I want to make about my small geographical place in this huge scheme of things called life, in terms of family, in terms of voices, it was [the still unpublished] *Mfua's Song*. And it was a work of labor that lasted some twenty years, and part of it's still in progress. The great advantage of being an African American is that you can invent yourself any way you want to. And I had no desire to run away from my roots, in terms of family.

Trying to see slavery as a kind of a testing ground, a proving ground—somehow my story had to come clear through it. And then how would I pass it down? I don't know if the story would have had the meaning that it did, had it not been for slavery. Maybe I would have taken the tale for granted. But it took a great deal of difficulty for the people to live their lives and then have someone to tell those tales, for them to get passed down. And more in terms of life work—because you don't need to publish a five-hundred-page poem—although maybe you need to write it. I'm debating this—what does it prove? I'm not trying to prove anything. But the only thing that I know is that I might be in a position to put it in print. There will be a version of it in print while I'm alive. The whole thing.

RG: Speaking of those tales that you could pass on, I'm still thinking about those two that you told me about your grandfather. What do you take those two stories to mean—the school story and the horse story? How do you read those?

SP: In many ways it could be a microcosm of both slavery and the postbellum constrictions placed on black humanity. On the one hand, the one role that could have led my grandfather away from the plow to something in another land would have been literacy, and that's cut off. So he's doomed to work with his hands, to work the land, for the rest of his life. But his mother, feeling that spirit in him that would not allow the woman teacher to unjustly hit him on his ear—rather than have that broken—felt that whatever the consequences of this immediate thing, somehow he would be able to negotiate the rest of his life, because she wouldn't whip him.

The other one, it's the personal toughness of the blues. Hell, you don't let no such thing as no broken bones stop you from being a determined man, there ain't no need to cry out for a doctor, you made a mistake, you going to grit your teeth and bear it. It's the toughness. He was a self-made man who had nothing but his good name. Nothing but his good name.

RG: Telling tales in the poem is very different from telling them in fiction. In the poem, you're working with the language, not just the tale.
SP: I suspect that I will do some novellas on some blues singers. This needs to be preserved, to be put into a different form.

History and Imagination

SP: The fact that my ancestors made their entrance into the West via a slave ship does not present a problem for me such that I would regret my existence now. So in that sense, slavery doesn't bother me. But I suppose that the more I look at it, the more I doubt that the reason why Africans were enslaved was because they were black and because the slavers thought they were inferior. The Africans were *there*, they *could* be enslaved, and the slavers felt they could *function* as slaves.

RG: So you see it in more materialist and economic terms, or even class terms, rather than in racial terms?
SP: Yes. But I do feel that there is a great deal of anti- . . . or to put it another way, I do feel that the white imagination in Europe is *burdened* with the absence of humanity in blackness. I do feel *that*. Now that's different from the people who are *in* slavery. That attitude of the slavers might very well be their justification, as they saw it, and may very well be their ignorance. Black people were expert in planting rice—and slavers knew that. Slaves were brought over here simply to plant rice. In South Carolina and North Carolina. They were expert in horses, and many of them in working in metals.

RG: So you see slavery as kidnapped semiskilled labor.
SP: Often *skilled* labor.

RG: Clearly they were kidnapped for their economic value in building white fortunes. And the racism?

SP: It looks like it comes as an explanation of why they did it. A justification on the part of the intellectual. The intellectual did not write a treatise except after the fact. There *is* racism. But I'm trying to say that if the slaves had been impractical, and black folks had not had the skills that were needed to build a society, it wouldn't have gone anywhere.

RG: I once heard you speak on a panel about class, and I wanted to ask you how you saw that issue in African and African American history, and what it was about class that compelled your imagination.

SP: What compelled my imagination is that I am a descendant of the slaves who were involved in agriculture. My entire imagination, at least in terms of my roots, as far back as I can go, is with my people, who were those who worked the land, principally cotton, and that's how they survived. But I also knew that in my family there were those who had mixed heritage, so consequently they did different jobs. One of my great-uncles was a fireman—his father was white, so he was a fireman. My father worked the cotton field. Class in this society creates the choices for you, not color.

I don't think that a poor white youth accused of rape has the same chance that a Kobe Bryant has. Kobe Bryant has historical notions of racism against him; pertinent to the black male there is a whole history of the desire for white women and what that implies. But he's got the bourgeoisie representing him. So when the lawyers come on behalf of Kobe, they're going to come with bad intentions. They will come to destroy the victim. They've got the means to do the kind of investigation to nullify the claim, which means to destroy. When this happened with O. J. Simpson, people did not understand it. It was the first time that you had American law against someone black and yet the bourgeoisie was the defendant. And they come with bad intentions. Even the evidence is not evidence. They can hire better witnesses than the government can locate. Even the timeline can't work, because they can hire experts to destroy it. If you don't have the resources, whatever the story is, it goes unchallenged. You get better trained people defending than they've got prosecuting. That's what I thought in the O. J. Simpson case. Very early I did not think that Marcia Clark had any business prosecuting against people who should have been judging her when she passed the bar. She was out of her class. Completely. Out of her class in terms of the law, in terms of jury selection, and definitely in terms of literacy—how you explain it. You can recall Anita Hill had accused Clarence Thomas of sexual harassment—but Clarence Thomas had the bourgeoisie defending him. And when the white feminists came after him—Arlen Specter and Orrin Hatch and some of those sons destroyed them, completely annihilated them. Because they had that *badge* of owning the law. And although they are not concerned about what has happened with black men, obviously they were able to deflect all the criticism that the feminists would have had against him. I thought that O. J. Simpson benefited in a very crazy way from some of that—it's hard to really prosecute a black man vis-à-vis a white woman without raising certain issues of fairness.

So now, being in the university, you see class issues, also. This is more apparent if you look at African American faculty—their politics are often determined more by their class concerns than by their color. The more prestigious the university they went to, and the more prestigious the professor they had—why, some of them are more elitist than a grandchild of George W. Bush will be, in terms of what they think the academy should do, or who they think the academy is there for. They are very concerned that they bring in professors like them, who are paid like top professors, but that concern may not trickle down to bringing in some black kids who are like them and making sure that those kids, who are having all kinds of problems, can get through. In fact, more than likely, they talk more about who should be here than other people.

RG: A Clarence Thomas syndrome?
SP: But Clarence Thomas is not alone. Politically, you cannot get an audience with the bourgeoisie if you question meritocracy. If you question that whole system you don't go too far with the bourgeoisie.

There is a dual dilemma presented to one, if one is African American, and it is precisely this: first, that our forcible introduction to the West via the Atlantic was an introduction in which we did not have humanity, nor did we have the rights that any citizen would have had in any state in the country, since we were property, since we were chattel. Now I'm simply speaking of the process. Then second, there's another process of acculturation, whereby, beginning with capture, through incarceration in the slave castle on the coast of West Africa, through the horrible middle passage ordeal across the Atlantic, through the auction block, through seasoning, and through essentials of enslavement, where there's a dialogue between the cultures that Africans brought with them, which were being destroyed, and their contact with the West. And the *culture* of the West and the Western

heritage did not own the slave ship. The literature of the West existed inde-
pendently of the slave ship. So that if the literature of the West is outstanding and excellent *prior* to the slave ship, it definitely would be valid and
great *after* the slave ship. The identity of people like myself whose ancestors
came over on slave ships is neither African nor European, so it would be
truly American. This new identity is formed here, and I suppose that culturally it would be from remnants, from survivals of African culture, somehow
syncretized, intricately dialogued, with Western notions of culture. So the
African American, it seems to me, would be the true American.

RG: Ellison says something like that, doesn't he?
SP: Yes, he does.

RG: But there are scholars who have said that the literature before the slave
ship already has in it the attitudes and assumptions about human beings,
culture, and race that make slavery possible. That is to say, that the literature, too, is compromised—as when Edward Said points out that the completely domestic novels of Jane Austen have in their distant background the
slave/sugar trade. What do you think?
SP: It's a great idea, but it's not consistent with what I have come to learn
about the slave trade. The Portuguese began to take slaves from West Africa,
bringing them to the New World. The data suggest that the Europeans' initial foray into West Africa was for El Dorado, was for gold not slaves. And to
solve this increasing problem of labor in the New World, their first impulse
was Native Americans, not Africans.

They even tried indenturing Europeans, but if *they* ran away, they could
change their identity. And you're talking about a society in West Africa with
a long heritage of agriculture, a tropical climate, a settled life—one of the
arguments given against Native Americans being slaves was that they were
nomadic and could not handle that. So I would reason that the Africans
were there, and in great numbers, and the Europeans invented a rationale
for enslaving them. And I don't know if the slave traders ever read Jane Austen. They might have, but I don't know that.

I don't think that slavery invalidates the greatness of Western literature.
I don't think that the fact that some people may have used literature to jus-
tify slavery invalidates it. I still think that part of my heritage as an African
American is Western literature. And I think Western literature is a great
tool that one can use to affirm and celebrate one's humanity.

RG: You said the other day in passing, "How can I take any of the faces out of the mirror?"

SP: There are far more faces when I look at myself, in terms of my history, if I want to look at it chronologically. Not every slave who made his way to the New World had to be captured by Europeans. There were also some black folks playing minimal roles. That's number one. Number two, my genetic pool has been democratized with Native Americans and Europeans, so when I look in the mirror, I'm not simply the generic dark African. There is far more evidence of my connection to people of Asian descent, and Native Americans, and a lot of people of European descent. And I have no need to take any of that out of the mirror, or to go to war with any of that. The fact of the matter is, I have a complex history; I have a complex genetics, and I have a complex culture. And somehow I have to pattern my way out of that to some kind of vision that would allow me to make sense of my existence.

On Reading and Teaching

SP: The greatest indictment that Ellison made against Wright is that he put no characters in any of his short stories that were as intelligent as Richard Wright. So part of the problem that I suppose I was having was that I was not the bluesman—I was not educated that way, so what then do I do with my literacy? Is it criminal to have literacy?

RG: In whose eyes?

SP: I always admired the poets who were gifted with language, from Homer to Milton. The ones that I didn't think were gifted with language I stayed away from. And I'm talking about the distinctive mastery of a variety of forms. Looking at twentieth-century American poetry, and looking at the body of the work, I think that T. S. Eliot and Gwendolyn Brooks produced phenomenal achievements. I'm talking about the distinctive mastery of a variety of forms. People can intellectualize this all they want, but for a poet, they were models of what I wanted to do. What they *did* was not what I wanted to do, but I had literacy, and how can I be true to myself as someone literate? They pushed me into being a poet who was really concerned with inventing and reinventing language in order to make his statement.

RG: You said, "Is it criminal to be literate?" Criminal in whose eyes?

SP: Look, there is no canon open enough to have a concept of *complete* literacy. Let me deal specifically with the tradition that I am born into. I think there are a number of tragedies. Paul Laurence Dunbar is a dialect poet. I thought that the poems not in dialect surpassed the poems in dialect. Someone feels that because you are an African American you are more appealing and can represent yourself and your folks better by writing in dialect—that becomes the lingua franca of African American poetry. Or if you look at the Harlem Renaissance, while it's true you're looking at a genius in Langston Hughes, who was expressing many of the experiences of everyday citizens of Harlem, what room then is there for Jean Toomer, who is singing about the depth of spirituality? Who lionizes him?

RG: And Sterling Brown is trying to say something *about* this by writing poems in both dialect and standard English?

SP: I think Sterling Brown is saying something about this in another way. Sterling Brown's great contribution to American poetry is that he *balladizes* his blues. For Sterling Brown, for all practical purposes, the blues has become a ballad. "Slim in Hell." And you're right—he is bilingual: he writes exquisitely in both traditions. He's a major poet, right there with Brooks and Hughes and Robert Hayden, and with Robert Frost and anybody else.

I do feel one thing very strongly. I taught at the university for thirty-one years. I don't believe people should ever teach writing if they are not engaged in trying to produce it at the highest level. As for reading, there are multiple texts always out there, and you need to present enough so people can begin to see how texts have been invented, and maybe that will help them in the process. There is no one particular text that people need to know. There are an awful lot of great texts—but it's not up to me to preserve the canon.

Here's what I always thought about the great writers: the only way you can say that you respect them is to try to out-write them. I love Neruda. I love Langston Hughes. And when I say "out-write" I don't mean imitate. You try to find your voice and exploit its potential, and the quest to say something that leads to the dignity of the human spirit. . . . You know, poetry is no different now than it was in 1845.

RG: Really?

SP: No. Americans don't know who the hell the important poets are. And definitely do not know what the canon will look like five years from now, let alone a hundred years from now. Everyone thought that Emerson would be the great American poet. It was Whitman. In other words, you need to allow poets to live and do their work and then you study them. That's what I always felt when I picked the pen up. You do the best you can, and if you do not say anything, you have not committed a crime. But to be concerned about what *Poetry* magazine or what any awards signify is irrelevant. But I knew that, though. I knew that nobody gave Charlie Parker and Dizzy Gillespie permission to invent bebop. Although I always privilege Parker and Gillespie as the brilliant proponents of bebop, nevertheless I'm cognizant of the remarkable achievements of Thelonius Monk, Bud Powell, Charlie Mingus, Max Roach, Art Blakey, and many others. Bebop represents a spectrum, and I am deliberately privileging the part of that spectrum that is Charlie Parker and Dizzy Gillespie. I knew that ten years after they died you couldn't talk about jazz without talking about bebop. I think that you create what you create, and either it influences, or it can influence, depending upon whether it is promulgated or not. But a poet's task is not to promulgate his work to an audience, but to promulgate his work to the publisher. Beyond that I don't think a poet can do anything else.

Now, what's odd about my experience is that I come up almost entirely immersed in a folk culture. Then all of this Western and world literature that I had to read, it might have taken a while for the poetic imagination to germinate in all of that. And it seems that the boundaries between what I think about black literature and Western literature dissolved when I worked on *Johannesburg* and *Ornate with Smoke*. My imagination selected what it wanted to select. It suggested to my *ear* the direction I should be going in. Also, I wondered why, since the use of language is such an art in African American experience, why didn't African American experience try to exploit how you could use language in poetry? I'm still wondering. The poet who did it, albeit in a modernist tradition, was Melvin Tolson. One way of doing it.

RG: Another of the poets who could master a variety of forms. An Armstrong.
SP: A genius. See, I'm black. Obviously the black aesthetics, black cultural nationalism, doesn't bother me, because I always thought that the best of African American art was what I aspired to do. And I always thought that the best of African American art was highly inventive. It required virtuosity. What Leon Forrest told me—and I don't know how much it influenced my poetry—is, "Plumpp, what you do is you take your blackness and your folk experience, let it dialogue with the books that belong on the shelf, and let your imagination run wild." [laughing] And that is essentially what I did. . . .

The idea of great poets—I don't know. I don't know how many poets who have lived in the twentieth century I think would be candidates for greatness. I do know that I can count all the ones I know on one hand and have some fingers left.

RG: That's not very many!

SP: There might be more. But I don't know. The poets that I thought would have to be unusually gifted and dedicated to create that body of work, American poets, right at the top of my list, for different reasons, would be T. S. Eliot and Gwendolyn Brooks. I thought they were poets, they had the muse—they listened to the muse. The other poet was Pablo Neruda.

RG: You said that you admired poets who had shown a mastery of a variety of forms.

SP: That's right. But as poets, not because some critic has said so, but as a matter of their apprenticing themselves to the traditions of poetry. But having said that, in many ways I think that the most important poet of the twentieth century in America is Langston Hughes, because he introduces this rich African American vernacular to poetry in a dignified way. I'm not sure he is the person who developed it to its highest level, but the mere fact that he introduced it means that you cannot overlook him when you look at twentieth-century poets. Among poets generally, you would have to look at them over centuries and see what their contributions really were. I'm fairly certain that in Neruda, Brooks, and Hayden I'm seeing poets whose mission in life was to sing and who learned to sing with perfection. Eliot had the advantage of being the most erudite, taking on very difficult topics, including history itself, poetry itself. And Neruda was the most spiritual, I felt.

RG: Despite his great success as a poet of the material world?

SP: You don't write *Macchu Picchu* without being spiritual. It comes through. And Brooks reclaimed and found some value in formal poetics in the middle of the twentieth century. It looks like she revitalized the ode and the sonnet—at least to me.

RG: And she reinvented herself.

SP: A couple of times. But Brooks was always singing in her own voice. It's a tragedy for someone who always looked at the black community, that people would try and look at her poetry *between* her pre- and her post-black periods. Her *consciousness* had absolutely nothing to do with the *content* of her poetry before she discovered the meaning of blackness for herself in 1967. In fact, I would argue that there are no better social commentaries on African American conditions in life than *A Street in Bronzeville* [1945] and *The Bean Eaters* [1960]. I would argue that, passionately.

RG: To make a distinction between her formal work and her free verse is superficial, in that sense.

SP: But then again—I find it ironic that the poem that she chose to end her last collection with was "In the Mecca," not one of her free-verse poems. "In the Mecca" combines the best of *A Street in Bronzeville* and *The Bean Eaters*. That is, the establishment of characters by using classical prosody, the rhyme scheme . . .

With Brooks, you're looking at a genius, although I think that people misread *Annie Allen* [1949]. I think that in *Annie Allen* Brooks is taking this form of poetic structure—meter, rhyme scheme, ballad, and mock-epic form—she is doing the same thing with those structures, in terms of her virtuosity, that Charlie Parker was doing with the alto sax solo. People don't see the virtuosity. And the virtuosity in and of itself is a commentary on what she thought about black life. People don't see that.

RG: By prizing virtuosity, by making it a cultural and moral and artistic value in itself, that's part of her commentary?

SP: It's part of the commentary.

RG: Or should I say, by *acknowledging* virtuosity? For it's not that she's imposing it on anybody; instead, she's working in a spirit akin to Parker's. *Annie Allen* is a bebop book, you're saying?

SP: There have been poetic texts that have achieved the Pulitzer Prize since *Annie Allen*, but there have not been any poetic texts that have achieved the Pulitzer since *Annie Allen* that have surpassed *A Street in Bronzeville* in terms of technical brilliance.

RG: That virtuosity itself is one form of her commentary is interesting—one can see in American poetry in general, and in the times of the Black Arts Movement, that one side demonizes virtuosity.

SP: It's sometimes demonized in the white world, too. But the problem with the Black Arts Movement was that they wanted utilitarian poetry; they wanted a kind of poetry that would dialogue with the consciousness of the oppressed masses, wherever the oppressed masses were—they wanted a *functional* kind of art, for the lack of a better word. And that would negate the poet's ability to make a commentary about black life simply through the handling of language, rather than doing it thematically.

RG: When you step into the classroom as a teacher, how does all that come into the process between you and your students?

SP: At two levels. It's simple. Literature as we know it is defined by its great texts. It's defined by its canonic texts. I'm speaking of Western literature. Now, I would support the idea that the canonic texts are somewhat more diverse than either the University of Illinois or Northwestern would admit. But it's just that simple. There is no other way—great literary texts from the *Iliad* and the *Odyssey* and the Bible, down to the twentieth century—to find literature. That's what the standards are; that's what the definition of literature is. Now, this process of one apprenticing oneself to Western literature is complex because people are individuals. I think it's too fashionable for one simply to go to school and say, I want to take an MA or MFA or PhD in literature and I want to be a writer. This might not be the way great writers are made. There's evidence that Faulkner got a great deal of information and technique from reading the Bible and listening to people. The writer, the one who uses his imagination and through narration creates a valid vision of the world, might be too complex for any syllabus.

At another level, though, I do feel that if any apprentice, any student, or any would-be writer can begin to see the brilliance of a great writer and begin to discern simply at a technical level how that was achieved, then one is well on his way to knowing the difficult task of creating some kind of a manuscript that would deserve to be on the bookshelf. I try to get students to read literature, to pay attention to it, on the one hand, and on the other hand, to see that there's only one standard for literature, and that is the production of a manuscript at the highest level, that would be in print one day. There is no other goal. Anything else, I think, is a waste of time. That is never easy. The idea that literature should be simple, should be for the people—the people don't need bad literature any more than they need bad food!

On Writing

RG: Did one of your books, either *Johannesburg* [1993] or *Ornate with Smoke* [1997], make you feel that you had turned a corner, changed something, discovered something new in your work? It seems to me that in *Ornate with Smoke* there is a manner, a method, a certain difference in your playfulness, that is your fuller mature artistic presence.

SP: I think *Ornate with Smoke* represents my imaginative approach to investigating unexplored places for language—both within the literary tradition, my cultural tradition, and what I could learn from playing with language as great jazz musicians had learned to play and discover methods of playing and hearing music by being playful. You know, technically, the most important book is definitely *Ornate with Smoke*. Now, *Johannesburg and Other Poems* is more or less a geography, a linguistic and metaphoric geography of my major concerns as a poet. They are the profound religious spirit, belief, and putting one foot forward every day until a million miles have been achieved, that I gather from my grandparents, who reared me, and that they gathered from their parents and grandparents, who were slaves. And that's in the southern landscape. Maybe "Sanders Bottom" metaphorically represents my attempt to almost take the freedmen as slaves—but this time in bondage to circumstance, bondage to family, and just through the sheer ability to live and believe, to endure, to achieve longevity. There's a song. That's one part.

The Chicago part of my imagination and concern is represented by blues and jazz—although blues and jazz are on a continuum, with me. The way I view it, had I been born in 1870 in Mississippi, with a third-grade education by 1890 or 1895, I'd have been singing the blues. But if my brother had been born at the same time and had matriculated at one of the black colleges, I think he would have picked up the trumpet. He would have had more access to the European world, and he would have been able to inner-visualize *his* voice as an African American by almost inventing an African American tradition *out of* a Western tradition.

My other concern: I'm an American who realizes that Africa is a *continent* my ancestors come from. And my sense of social justice is perhaps represented by South Africa. The conditions in South Africa are analogous in many ways to the experience of African Americans. They were the majority of people who had their lands expropriated and controlled because of gold and diamonds; we had our labors expropriated for the sake of cotton, tobacco, and sugar cane. The big difference is, we had the advantage of living in rectangular houses, known as "shotgun"; in South Africa, they had not discovered the rectangle, so that the houses were square and were called "matchbox" houses. That's one thing. The other aspect of it is that you have the African sensibility, concerning the most technically advanced society on the continent—you have that in South Africa and you have that here. You're singing songs in Zulu and Setswana, and all of a sudden you are uprooted and you're in Jo'berg or Capetown, and somehow your folk culture gets transformed into a music that I think is jazz—so it's a highly improvisational music, like jazz.

Yet another aspect of it is, the trade union movement radicalizes whatever politics that exist. It did so when blacks moved to Detroit and Chicago—you get the Communist Party USA, sleeping-car porters; you get Richard Wright, you get William Attaway. The same thing is true in South Africa. You get an urban proletariat, for the lack of a better word, that is exploited, and from that, some incidents spark and you begin to get a national leadership. It occurred in South Africa after World War II, maybe in 1948, and it occurred in the United States around 1955 with Martin Luther King. So 1991 in South Africa was when I began to understand how individuals fight for social equality, human dignity, and justice; how they fight with ideas; how they fight by enduring; and how they fight to set up a society free of racialism. How they fight to set up a society where there is no lingering need for retribution.

So that's my idea. I see that in South Africa, and in confronting South Africa and trying to write about it, particularly the long poem "Johannesburg," I was challenged because at once I, too, was attacked—my *sensibility* was being attacked, although I'm not sure that those in power were aiming to hit me, in particular. I so identified with the South Africans when I heard the shots at night, when I heard the curses, when I saw the dead bodies; I saw the subservience that one had to adhere to under apartheid—you know, maybe I was in the back seat . . .

Because African Americans are a black minority vis-à-vis white people in the United States, the word "black" is thrown around too loosely. But in South Africa, you only have four million whites and you have about twenty-seven million Africans and maybe four or five million coloreds, so that . . . whites definitely did not walk the streets of Johannesburg at night like they owned it. They didn't drive down Lake Shore Drive. They had twenty-five-foot walls around their houses, steel bars at their doors, so it's another world, and then you see all this poverty. It's almost as if when I was in South Africa I was at a long period of mourning and crying, and the sunrise of laughter was just over the hill. Whatever that thing called "history," that thing called "oppression," "minority rule"—whatever that is, it was about to break. The dam was about to break. There was a great deal of hope in the eyes of people. Their body language. It was over. They had not voted yet, but it was over. You got that feeling. And they had strong leadership, out-standing leadership—they did not need one individual. Mandela is a great man, but Tambo did a yeoman's job of taking the organization into exile and bringing it back. There were a lot of strong leaders. It's surprising, but there were a large number of whites supporting the ANC, within the coun-try—like Nadine Gordimer. I suppose at one level I saw all of what I thought about hope and human justice. But by the time I go back in 1995—I have not written about that.

RG: Between *Johannesburg* and *Ornate with Smoke,* those kinds of things left your poems as the subjects and titles, but are still in the texture; how-ever, you turned a little and started looking at the jazz man, the sax man, and you became fascinated by the individual. In *Johannesburg* you seem fas-cinated by the *city* of individuals. Something like that? What produced that change in you? What did that feel like?

SP: I don't know how conscious I was, but for a very long time—when I was somewhere between twenty-two and twenty-three, in Chicago, and saw all this culture that's here, the first thing I wanted to do was to see my heroes, so I saw Howlin' Wolf; I saw Muddy Waters. I was here permanently—I was here to *live*—by 1962. And the thing that struck me about blues singers, that I had never really articulated before, was that they sang with the same kind of idiom and the same kind of pain [as] my uncles, my grandfathers, and the men folks I knew on the farms—that that was where they had come from, that they had not done anything to *change* that language; they had found a way of making *art* out of *it*. I was fascinated with how they could move peo-ple, similar to the way that the black ministers can move people in revivals, or how the black minister can console families at funerals, how they could use words that had that much power to transform what is inside individuals.

RG: Did the culture require you to make a choice between the black minis-ter and the jazzmen—I know they weren't necessarily the same.

SP: But you're a strange creature when you're black and educated. It's almost like you've got passports to all of the world. You're *literate*—so in the jazz club you had to dress, you had to observe the manners that were expected, but that's where the educated middle-class black people were. I can remember seeing Wynton Kelly, piano, Philly Joe Jones, drums, Paul Chambers, bass, Kenny Dorham on trumpet. It's the playing; it's the playing! See, it's a long time before you understand what's focusing the particular articulation of the trumpet—but it was that man on those drums, and that bass, all of them working together—Good Lord! Paul Chambers was one of the great, great bass players. I'm hearing it, and it looked like he was pushing the man on the piano, and it's somehow as if the jazz musician had established a kingdom replete with subjects on that stage! [laughing] He was a man, right? But I'm still this black boy in this white world. It dawned on me—the true greatness of jazz men . . .

I saw Sonny Stitt; I saw all of them. I wanted to see Thelonius Monk, and there was a club in Old Town called The Plugged Nickel, at Clark and Division, and so I went up to the club, dressed in my best Esquire tie. I think I had on a blue blazer, gray trousers, black loafers, blue socks [laughing]—tried to look as educated and inconspicuous as I could—I was black and that's what you do. When you're black and educated, you're in this integrated world, you have to relish those moments. And a funny thing happened. I was sitting there, had not even finished my first drink, and I heard this commotion at the door, and I turned—and there was this black man, he had on what looked like a hunting jacket and a hunting cap like they used to wear in the South, eyes red, wild-eyed [laughing], and all of a sudden he decided to enter, and he entered. He bumped into white folks and spilled their drinks, and I flinched and began to say, What in the hell is going on? [laughing] and then he ran and jumped up on the stage and danced a jig! [laughing] He turned around three times and hit the piano and played for an hour without stopping. Thelonius Monk.

RG: That was Monk?

SP: I couldn't believe it. It dawned on me that you have to be great to do that. Not to alienate. To bring it off. [laughing]

That *band* was *there* when he hit that piano, man. It looked like he was dancing—I don't know if you ever watched him—he looked like he was dancing when he was playing the piano, with his whole body.

And for a long time I was fascinated. Even when I was trying to write about blues, I was wondering, what in the world is *making* these people? So a number of things led me back to jazz.

Maybe the three people who had the greatest influence on me were James Baldwin—because the very first thing I read by James Baldwin was "Sonny's Blues," a brilliant short story about how the musician could create that world, despite being maybe an ex-addict; it was a *world*. I think Sonny was a drummer, and he was into that *world*. Then, I suppose there are sections of Baldwin's *Another Country* [1962? 1968?] where Rufus and Vivaldo are smoking, and maybe Bird is playing, and he said all the squares had left—there's something about the people who listen to that music that is in my imagination.

Now, I confront jazz and poetry initially—although some people speak of Langston Hughes—in the bebop rendering of blues by Amiri Baraka, because of his ellipsis, his quick phrasing, his ability to integrate all kinds of art elements into a poem, particularly in *The Dead Lecturer* [1964] and *Preface to a Twenty Volume Suicide Note* [1961]. Then I'm trying to understand it, but there's something that Ralph Ellison says about Louis Armstrong—he said Louis Armstrong made poetry out of invisibility.

You know how you look at Louis Armstrong, the big teeth, and you don't hear what a genius he was in phrasing and singing. He played two instruments, and he played one instrument better than he played the trumpet, and that was his voice.

I don't know whether it was growth or not, but somewhere around 1980 I went out to a place called Enterprise Lounge and saw Von Freeman play tenor saxophone. The tenor saxophone reminds me of the human voice, and because I could sit so close and because of his manner of playing—you go there at 10:30, he'll start playing and sometimes he would play till 12:30 without stopping. It is not so much the way he was running the chromatics, but it was the way he was imposing his will on it, stretching out, sometimes staying within, the tradition. I took all these notes.

RG: In the club?

SP: In the club. And when I got back home. And somewhere twelve or fifteen years later, those notes became *Horn Man*. But the difference there is that there still was a concept of boundary of what I thought you could do with language, in *Horn Man*. I needed someone who could open up the door to Bird and beyond, for me. I'm not a musician—God knows I'm not a musician—but I can tell you right now that I heard no one in jazz who was as good as Charlie Parker and Dizzy Gillespie. They're another world; they were in another world conceptually, and it's unthinkable that anybody would try to challenge them technically. Bird was as good on his instrument as Isaac Stern was. Now, Fred Anderson played for me an interview that was done with Charlie Parker, in the mid-1940s. It completely blew my mind, and confirmed what I thought was happening. This interviewer said, "Bird, are you surprised that you invented bebop?" And Charlie Parker said, "No." He said, "In the three to five years before I invented bebop, I practiced eleven to fourteen hours a day." So this jazz musician is not some kind of freak of nature. The great jazz musicians are artists at the highest level, because they completely mastered their craft, and they are visionaries in terms of the language of music.

I asked Fred, "You don't ever play Bird." He said, "I don't ever play anybody but Fred." [laughing] I asked him, "What about bebop?" He said, "There were *tendencies* in bebop. Bebop wasn't one thing." He said it's true that Bud Powell, Charlie Parker, and Dizzy Gillespie heard things in a similar way. But he said that Thelonius Monk heard things in a different way. Mingus in an entirely different way. So you got bebop and people knowing they are on horns going differently. He said that the music had to *continue* to be creative.

Fred is seventy-four, and he said something that struck me—he said, "When I used to work, when I used to play regular, I used to practice eight hours a day." At that time he was about sixty-nine or seventy. I said, "How many hours you practicing now?" He said, "I don't have that much time, I don't do but three or four hours a day." And in fact when I took him the book [*Ornate with Smoke*], the club was closed, and I heard the tenor saxophone—he and his saxophone in there talking to the walls.

As a symbol of how the African sensibility survives the kind of bombardment that was an attempt to crush the African in slavery, it seemed to me that it was the jazz musician who put the Humpty Dumpty of the diasporic experience back together again.

RG: It sounds like in addition to admiring the genius, you admire the sheer and ferocious work ethic.

SP: I come out of a culture where work was praised, and I saw people who wanted to become athletes who would practice three different shifts a day—they would practice eight hours in the morning, eight hours during the day, and then they would go to the gym and practice eight hours again at night, playing basketball! The thing, I suppose, that bothers me is when people suggest that black athletes dominate sports because of their innate physical characteristics—I don't buy that. From a very early age, if you're an African American athlete, you play against the very best athletes in the world. What happens in more "civilized," "higher" classes is that twelve-year-olds play against twelve-year-olds, and they play *like* twelve-year-olds. What happens if you're from the community I come from—hell, if you can take the ball to the hoop against somebody twenty, you do it. Because of the skill level. And I think that's what makes pro basketball—the skill level. Even in my day you couldn't take the ball inside. No, they would get up there and slap it back. People like Dr. J and Michael Jordan need every trick that they've got to get that ball off against these black boys—otherwise they'll slap it back at them. People don't look at it from that angle—they should say, "He *needed* to be that good—not when he was in the pros, but when he was out there on the court."

So I suppose I admire discipline. I thought that there was a great deal of discipline in the people who were being sold, who were being beaten, who were being executed, who ran away, and who in the face of all that, could produce a classic like "Nobody Knows the Trouble I've Seen" or "Sometimes I Feel like a Motherless Child." There's a discipline, there's a faith and a discipline somewhere, to create that. It dawned on me how good you have to be to play with Duke Ellington. That's why Charlie Parker and the others were so good—the standards of playing with the big band were so high. You already had to be great to play it. It's that kind of discipline that's the best of both the African American and the American traditions.

RG: Something in your work that starts in *Johannesburg* and *Horn Man* and comes into its full force in *Ornate with Smoke* looks like a very disciplined freedom, a very practiced art of improvisation. An artistic paradox. You keep *turning* the language, over and over. The poems in *Ornate with Smoke* move episode by episode; you turn it and turn it. Each time it's moving a little, and then sometimes it seems to explode for six or seven lines—all the puns, all the line breaks, everything almost sets off a little explosion. But you keep turning it, you don't let it go, you don't stop a poem where someone else might at a nice ending; you're always pushing it further.
SP: Because I think I have a musical analogy. I think that linguistically I feel that the language in the poem should be pushed the way musical concepts are pushed in bebop and now pushed in this highly improvisational jazz. The other thing that I discovered—you don't know anything about yourself when you start—was that I could *hear language.*

RG: You are a poet of the ear?
SP: I could hear language. In other words, when I first was writing, and I had a double or triple entendre, it was like an accident, but then I found out that I was *hearing* that. I had not intentionally set out to *do* that, but—

RG: But you heard it.
SP: I heard it. I said, I think I'm going to jot it down. My habit is to jot it down and put it on a computer. I really did not know what *Ornate with Smoke* looked like until Gwendolyn Mitchell [editor at Third World Press]

had organized all of the poems into a book. I didn't know. Likewise, I had this terrible feeling with *Velvet BeBop Kente Cloth* [2003]—are you writing *Ornate with Smoke* again? I know I wasn't, but you don't *know* [laughing]. The challenge of being a poet is to accept all this stuff that you don't know: you're going to trial and you don't know what your evidence is. You have to defend your life, and you don't know what your evidence is. And in the process of reading it some thirty times to try to catch all the errors, I suppose I saw the difference: in terms of idiom, the big difference is that the imagination in *Velvet BeBop Kente Cloth* is geared more toward dialogue. And narration. And *play*—with a lot of a musical concept, and exploiting a lot of the cultural history that comes out of diaspora—although I'm talking about bebop, I'm talking about Paul Bogle, who was a maroon leader. It didn't occur to me before, that probably the first poetry created by human beings was when they named themselves. So that begins a play with names—the collection of names in any language is a rare kind of poetry.

RG: I failed to mention *Blues Narratives* [1999]. In that book you already created two dialogues. Your mother and grandfather are not there to speak for themselves, but you create dialogue by creating alternating songs, although you continue to experiment with the line and the word, and that is important in your getting to *Velvet BeBop Kente Cloth.*
SP: *Blues Narratives* is really an excerpt from a much longer work, where I was trying to deal with my matrilineal lineage in an imaginative way.

RG: That's a very large book, still unpublished except for *Blues Narratives*, right?
SP: It's about seven or eight hundred pages. *Mfua's Song.* I had thought that somewhere between forty and sixty, if you had something that you really wanted to say, that you really wanted to attempt, that was very difficult, I thought that that was a good time to do it.

RG: Did you work on *Mfua's Song* for many years?
SP: Fifteen or so.

RG: And that was a separate project from the other books you were publishing at that time?
SP: I don't know anything about other poets, but for me, although I published some poetry in the 1970s, I suppose the full voice doesn't occur in my work till *The Mojo Hands Call, I Must Go*, which was already 1982. But then

I do not publish another book until 1989, and that's *Blues: The Story Always Untold*.

RG: Were you already working on *Mfua's Song* in that period?
SP: I was working on it. I was trying to figure out how I could narrate, and make Mfua real.

RG: Who is Mfua?
SP: I was told by an aunt of mine, who was born about 1878 and died about 1982 or '83—her name was Alberta—we were talking about family members and she told me about this woman by the name of Tympe. "She's one of your folks," she said. Tympe was born in 1772, and she died about 1908.

RG: That's an unbelievably long life.
SP: She was 135. She was a slave in North Carolina. The folks who owned her moved to Mississippi. She walked behind the ox cart and it took six months. That's what my aunt told me. Nothing else. What triggered my imagination, because I am a poet, was that Tympe had to have a mother. So I have her tell the story of her mother, who was Mfua. About how they came over on a ship. She narrates Mfua. My task was to get a name that sounded West African. Mfua's narrative. Then my maternal grandmother, who was 103 when she died, has a long narration. All of my uncles and aunts, my grandfather. The thing is, the poet's part begins in Mississippi, comes to Chicago, and then reverberates as the poet visits South Africa. So this poet's experience is reflected in what he sees when he goes to South Africa.

I have no way of knowing whether it's complete or not. Or how to pin it down, to work it in, but it's a particular narrative that allows me to construct history through family.

RG: What did you feel you had to do to make Mfua real?
SP: She's a woman—there are no slave narratives of women who came over on slave ships. There are very few slave narratives of women. What she would have faced. Her children around her. Since Tympe lived so long, she could tell that story; she would have seen it. At one point in the story, Tympe made a pact with the Mississippi River. In fact, they were suspicious of her because they would go down there and catch her talking to the river. They sold one of her sons. And so when the master's son went to the river, the river reached out and grabbed him and pulled him in. Voodoo-type

women. I suppose I thought that if the figure of Mfua couldn't exist, then the poem could not be written. Because Tympe got all of what she got from Mfua.

RG: I've read that poem in typescript and noticed that even though you began it long ago, your way of working with the line in later books was already there.

SP: The problem I have—people ask me, Why do you use the virgules? I'm breaking it right . . . I was hearing the *voice*. And vaguely I remember seeing ex-slaves and hearing them talk.

I was born in 1940, but there were people around in the 1940s who had been born in the 1840s and 1850s. You don't know they were slaves, because you don't go around saying this—it's not that important. But you hear them talking. What did I hear them say? [Plumpp says it in dialect pronunciation and then says it again in language closer to Standard English:] "Us didn't know chickens had nothing but heads and foots." You hear epigrammatic kinds of things. And you hear a use of anonymity to describe a person. They tell you about the horror without specifically identifying the victim. That's one of the techniques used by the old folks fluent in the living vernacular: "You know so-and-so had lied, and old master put that hide to her." The way they're speaking, it's almost like it was an instrument. If you are trying to capture the nuances of what they're saying, the rhythms of what they're say-ing, you almost have to deconstruct the sentence in order to illuminate the validity of the nuances of these speakers. I didn't know how to do it, at first. Because I write by ear. And by the same token, if you have a lot of slashes, then you can . . . How do you represent what you *hear* in language? I assume that because I write in longhand, I can force the reader to hear what I hear, and the comma is too subtle to do it. Sometimes you need a visual guide so you can hear something rhythmically.

RG: I remember that William Goyen, who wrote prose in the speech rhythms of white, East-Texas country people, said, "They got the speech, I got the voice." And thinking about your work, I thought, we all speak lan-guage, but some poets sing language. It's not that you have to write some-thing called a song, in a song form, but when you write the language you are singing it in a way instead of saying it. This might be of interest only to other poets, but I see you using the slash and the line-end to create not interruptions but a tiny hesitation and rhythmic syncopation to double the number of those effects by putting the slash inside the short line. I noticed that you did not do that in *Ornate with Smoke*, but you went back to it in *Velvet BeBop Kente Cloth*.

SP: It was not done as much, because I think *Ornate with Smoke* was a breakthrough kind of book that had me chasing these different languages around too much. Did I do what I was supposed to do? I was surprised that Keith Gilyard gave it a great review in *African American Review*. But he understood the tradition.

By the time I got to *Ornate with Smoke* and *Horn Man* [1995], it was clear to me that the best way for me to exploit my concerns with blues was to do it as a jazz voice. I don't necessarily have to do twelve-bar A-B blues. That was not the challenge for me.

RG: You wanted to do what the jazzmen do *with* the blues, instead of doing straight blues.

SP: That's what I wanted.

RG: *Blues Narratives* is more straight blues, and *Ornate with Smoke* and *Velvet BeBop Kente Cloth* are more like the jazzmen using the blues.

SP: That's right.

RG: How do you shape your poems as whole pieces? You typically not only shape a poem out of small pieces, but then you also shape a longer sequence out of individual poems.

SP: I have no concept of the printed page when I write. I write on napkins, backs of envelopes—

RG: I've seen you taking notes in a blues club, and I said to you, "I see that this is your French café," and you said, "That's right."

SP: I have to trust my ear. In fact, I don't even number the poems or say this is the beginning—the only poem that even had a title when I wrote *Ornate with Smoke* was the title poem. That's why you need someone who's a sensitive reader. The editor negotiates the poem from the poet's head to the public. One of the things that Gwendolyn Mitchell said is that the poems can be numbered—some with titles, some without—and she might have had some sense of how they should be ordered.

RG: She helped you create the shape of the big pieces?

SP: A lot of that is editing. As a poet, you have to hear whether people are trying to interpret something so that the literate public can understand. I thought that she got it. She knew the culture, she knew jazz, she had been through an MFA program, she knew workshopping. I deleted a few things if I thought they would present too many problems for readers. Because if I decide to publish it, I want it to be coherent enough for the reader to make his judgment. I have to trust to my ear when I write—that's why I write longhand. If I write longhand, I only know how a series of these pieces look when I put them down on the page. Then I have no idea what the book looks like till I've got it all there. And then when you have it all numbered right, you have a complete change of perception. Remember, for me it is just one long piece and none of the sections have titles. But the sections are designated by triple spaces in between.

RG: Not a short song but an aria. The long solo.
SP: Yeah. Why long? Maybe some of the things done in jazz, instruments dialoguing, something like that takes space. And although my poems are long, my lines are not long. For me the essence of the line is the importance of the word in the line.

RG: You do just about everything with a word that can be done.
SP: What can't be done, I'm going to do that, too. [laughing]
I'm sixty-three years old, right. And Haki Madhubuti might have asked me about putting together a volume of selected poems. And I told him: Your statement indicates that the poet is not doing something new. If I thought I was doing something that I was already doing . . . Let somebody else collect it after you die! I understand a "selected poems" as having a pedagogical reason.

RG: But also a publishing reason. Some of your books are out of print and in a selected volume they come back.
SP: I think I'll do it. But that was my thinking, because my imagination was different, now. This whole encounter with bebop completely changed what I thought you could do with language.

RG: The encounter with Von Freeman? 1982?
SP: 1981 or '82. But it doesn't become a reality in poetry until 1995. But I have published most of my poetry since 1993. *Johannesburg, Horn Man, Ornate with Smoke, Blues Narratives*, and *Velvet BeBop Kente Cloth*.

RG: And you wrote all of *Mfua's Song*?
SP: All written in the same period.

RG: I notice that Keorapetse Kgositsile said in his introduction to your chapbook *Steps to Break the Circle* [1974], "After a rally or demonstration, of what use are the picket signs?"
SP: That's true. But *music* has, I suppose, always intuitively been my model. And maybe I was always trying to achieve music at different levels—sometimes blues, sometimes jazz, sometimes Negro spirituals. But I wanted to take it beyond what I simply heard. Whatever it is that I heard, maybe I wanted to, in the words of Leon Forrest, take it and challenge it at the level of the imagination. To be some kind of literary device or literary concern. The problem I have is that I am double conscious. I am not someone who cannot read and write, dealing with the blues. I am someone dealing with the blues who has read a great deal of world literature. And there's no way in the world that I can amputate my literacy and still remain a poet. I cannot abort it. I cannot truncate it. I cannot get rid of it. So whatever literacy I have, I have to bring to bear on the blues. To come back to what you said, maybe that is why, in my later poetry, bebop and jazz become such central metaphors and symbols in my work—because I see that the importance of the breakthrough in bebop and jazz lies in the mastery of craft, at the individual level. Whereas in the movement, there is a suggestion that you can have art based on collective mastery. But the breakthroughs come through the quest for an individual voice that literally shows others how to do it.

RG: We're back to the epic hero. The heroes of the Iliad are not "the Greeks," but particular individuals.
SP: Odysseus endures for twenty years the wrath of the gods. He has a faithful wife and a faithful son. Maybe that's what I'm wrestling with; maybe I'm trying to find what the Greeks would call *aretê*. Maybe I'm trying to find some black *aretê*. Maybe that's what I see the task of the poet or writer is, to achieve that.

RG: The individual *aretê* in the context of the collective necessity and the collective enterprise?
SP: I don't know that I have a particular—I was pleased and stunned to see Mario, from the Guild Complex [a literary center in Chicago], when they performed *Velvet BeBop Kente Cloth*, they did it as rap.

RG: What did you think about that?

SP: I felt exonerated. Because I felt that if in fact you were a true rapper, you would look at music like bebop as a way out. And they automatically went there. Their ear—there's something about what I'm trying to do on the page, it's consistent with what they're trying to do when they speak. Because I don't speak my poems. I'm writing my poems. But we're dealing with the same tradition. So I felt exonerated in that sense. But also I think that if you don't reinvent yourself, I don't think you live, I think you breathe. At birth you get breath; at the time when you find your voice as a writer you begin to live. Reinvention is the dialysis machine of your art. Your literary kidneys will fail if you don't change and reinvent yourself in terms of technique. But that's personal. I like writers who are inquisitive and explore either ideas or language. Those are the writers I love.

RG: Well, that's Eliot, that's Brooks, and that's Neruda, poets whom you often praise.

SP: Those are the writers I identify with—not that I want to be like them; I don't want to do what they did. Somehow coming out of this vernacular, I don't know why I wanted to look at words, why I was so fascinated by words. For example, in *Velvet BeBop Kente Cloth*, there are a lot of names. Although at the time, maybe I was trying to play with the names, but it dawned on me that some of the greatest poems invented by human beings were names. That this idea of naming is a way of creating great poetry. Naming people, naming places, naming things, naming gods, naming attributes. And the other thing was this constant need in me to be an individual and to collect these fragments of my diasporic self and somehow pattern that. I'm not just an African American, I'm an Afro-Diaspora child.

RG: To collect the fragments of your diasporic self and—

SP: And pattern it somehow. I think that was the quest in *The Mojo Hands Call, I Must Go* [1982], in *Blues: The Story Always Untold* [1989] . . . And definitely the idea of the saxophonist riffing elaborate varied Kente cloth—the Kente cloth being something in Africa, but the idea was that you can take the sounds and conjure it into reality.

RG: I was going to ask you about "Clinton," in *The Mojo Hands Call, I Must Go*—which was an autobiographical poem—how would you tell the story of your development as an artist, in addition to what you say in that poem about people and places and political puzzles and dilemmas?

SP: In many ways, *Ornate with Smoke* began to deal with that complexity. The eloquence of the African American idiom and the formal legacy of Western literature, Western poetics and its potential to expand—somewhere between those boundaries you find what I'm trying to do. I've simply taken Whitman and Langston Hughes and given one a saxophone and the other a trumpet.

RG: How do you see what happened to get you from where you started to *Ornate with Smoke*, artistically?
SP: Artistically—my confrontation with revolution in South Africa. There's no glory in the killing, in the suffering. So you have got to get to the point where you have set up some structures. So now you can educate people to read and to produce poems, themselves. That led me to the analysis that I needed to challenge myself literarily. There were dead bodies. There had been Soweto. You have a black president in South Africa. What do these children have more than anything? They have a chance to become literate and define themselves and their world. So having this kind of literature that addressed them and their conditions—after seeing that, that disappeared for me; my need to write that kind of literature left me. I would have to figure out how to expand literature and the literary for myself after that point, in order to become relevant. My writing after *Johannesburg and Other Poems* drastically changed—that was a transforming event in my life. Seeing social conditions transformed led me right back to literature. What's different about the children growing up in South Africa is that they will not have to write Dennis Brutus's *Letters to Martha* [1968] or Keorapetse Kgositsile's *Places and Bloodstains* [1975]. Their literacy will allow them to reinvent themselves in a way that they don't have to write those poems addressed to the horrors of apartheid. And neither would this poet need to write that, anymore.

RG: Won't they still have to write poems about their poverty, the racism that is still there?
SP: But I'm not so sure—since they got control of the government they can develop policies that do something about that. Poets should fall across an entire spectrum. More than anything else, they will need to become major literary voices addressing whatever it is that they address. Maybe I felt that more than anything else: that the revolution prevented their development. What would have happened to a lot of those poets if they had been able to develop during their whole lives as poets, working on their craft, as artists?

[. . .] Take Thomas McGrath—he seemed the only poet to have the erudition and the literary imagination to say anything about the worker, the failure of workers' movements, the independent peasants, the legacy of Native Americans. The odd thing about him was that he had both the training and the literary imagination. I wanted to know, What would he have said if he had not had the training? What would he have said that would have remained? So the point I'm making is that I'm a post-apartheid poet. Telling me that there are homeless children in the streets of Johannesburg—you'll have to go somewhere else. I've heard that, I've seen that, don't tell me that in a poem today; don't go to Pimville Station [in Soweto], go somewhere else with your imagination, about human potential. You've got these kids, you've got control of education—you can educate them. Maybe what I'm saying is that the true revolutionary artist has to knock the door down with craft, at this particular time. Maybe that's what I'm saying. Maybe that's what I feel for myself; maybe that's what I feel the challenge is. I don't think the bourgeoisie has ever had no monopoly on craft! I don't think they have no ownership of it! They don't have no deeds to craft!

RG: They have a lot of control over what's disseminated but not over what's created?
SP: I suppose that my work after *Johannesburg* is my application for some of the deeds to craft.

RG: You said something earlier about how it took you awhile to understand what you were hearing before you could get it on the page. You were hearing two or three levels at once.
SP: I was hearing a pun that I didn't want to put down. Because I thought I was hearing too much.

RG: Every poet should be so lucky, or talented.
SP: I was hearing something else. In other words, the open-endedness was leading me to something I was hearing, but I was shutting down.

RG: But then you let it come through.
SP: I thought about what jazz musicians had been doing—where there had been space, the jazz musicians had been riffing into those spaces. And I said, I'm going to riff, to rip, into them.

Discussing *Velvet BeBop Kente Cloth* (TWP 2003) and the Writer's Vision: A Conversation between Dike Okoro and Sterling Plumpp

Dike Okoro / 2004

From *Reverie: Midwest African American Literature* 4 (2004): 1–7. Reprinted by permission of *Reverie*.

This interview was conducted in Professor Plumpp's office at Chicago State University on 22 March 2004.

Sterling D. Plumpp has published numerous books, including *Horn Man*; *Ornate with Smoke*; *Blues: The Story Always Untold*; *Half Black Half Blacker*; *Johannesburg and Other Poems*, edited the South African poetry anthology *Somehow We Survive*, and is the author of the recently published blues poetry collection, *Velvet BeBop Kente Cloth*. His numerous awards for literary and lectureship recognition include the Carl Sandburg Literary Prize and two Amoco-Silver Circle Award for excellence in teaching. Plumpp's work has been used for the 1991 Chicago Blues Festival and at an international gathering of artists in Cologne, Germany. In December 2001 he retired with emeritus status, having taught as a professor of English and African American studies at the University of Illinois at Chicago since 1971. Plumpp, a winner of the one-million-dollar Illinois lottery, is at present the Gwendolyn Brooks writer-in-residence at Chicago State University and a professor of creative writing/African American literature at the university's MFA program.

Dike Okoro: Your poems, according to John Edgar Wideman, "conduct a kind of research upon the body of blues tradition." Please shed some light on your early development as a writer and how that experience helped in enhancing your vision. In other words, when did you begin writing?

Sterling D. Plumpp: I began writing in my late adolescence and began using an alternate vision to what I was concerned with in my late childhood.

Okoro: Could you explain what you mean by an alternative vision?

Plumpp: As always, I suspect I wanted to craft reality to my vision, no matter what facade from reality suggested. I thought that when something becomes reality for me, it arises as alternative to reality.

Okoro: So when did you become interested in the writing as an art? In other words, as something you might use throughout your life?

Plumpp: I actually made the decision initially when I wanted to become a creative writer to mark the craft of literature and express myself sometime around the age of twenty or twenty-one. I had made that decision that would satisfy my curiosity and soul. And I made the decision to challenge myself to give back to literature as a writer, definitely, at the age of twenty-two.

Okoro: In your new book, *Velvet BeBop Kente Cloth*, you state what I consider a unique definition of the artist on page 62. Can you speak a bit on that?

Plumpp: I'd say that that is fairly close to what I'd consider a conjurer of both real and surreal. I wanted to start with something that is uniquely individual. That is to say that the writer sees the devices and ways of expression and he takes the mastery of the craft of his own voice, not the purpose for which it elicits. It is the idea behind the craft that we take seriously.

Okoro: Indeed an interesting way to look at the artist. You've published twelve books to date.

Plumpp: Yes.

Okoro: Of the twelve books, which gives you the most satisfaction?

Plumpp: In some ways I'd say *Blues Narratives*. Because at the time my mother died in 1980, a quarter of centuries were to pass after her death before I could actually dialogue with her and dialogue about her death in any meaningful and satisfactory way for myself. In terms of refereeing the writer, *Johannesburg and Other Poems* is fairly what I was drawing from, both thematically and geographically. *Ornate with Smoke* is the book that I think I found the possibility for my language.

Okoro: Staying on the point of you finding a possibility for your language, I'd say there is a sort of dialogue taking place in your poetry, which obviously evokes the use of vernacular among other musical devices. Therefore, would you say your poetry is a meeting ground for jazz, blues, and hip-hop?

Plumpp: In a sense, jazz, blues, and hip-hop in one way or the other are the most imaginative crafts that use the vernacular as a creative art, be it music, be it essay, be it poetry, be it fiction or nonfiction.

Okoro: Thanks. Let's look at tradition. Who are your major influences as a writer?

Plumpp: The writers who actually influenced me to write are the Greek playwrights Euripides and Aeschylus. But the individual whose life and work really allowed me to try to create a voice for myself was James Baldwin. And then the individual that allowed me to go back autobiographically to my roots in Mississippi, and who has made me to learn how to read meaning for meaning with suffering, was definitely Richard Wright.

Okoro: In that case, would you say Richard Wright is the writer whom you admire the most?

Plumpp: No. If I'd say the three writers that I admire the most, Ralph Ellison would definitely serve as one example. I admire and respect his penetrating essays on African American culture and experience and his brilliant execution of character and place in *Invisible Man*. It shows the eloquent perpetual for the African American writing utilized in African American themes. And the writer that I find the most inventive and the most masterful in fiction, without a doubt, is William Faulkner. I mean, I admire him for the virtuosity of *Absalom, Absalom!, Sound and the Fury*. It's just masterful. And the writer, I think, that really disturbed my soul, and I think that she did it because she wrote one of the two or three most important novels of the twentieth century, *Beloved*, is Toni Morrison.

Okoro: Let's now address a question I consider rather peculiar to this interview. Just how much power does the professional artist/writer have in a society such as America?

Plumpp: I think the writer's great power is to reject media, so that there is enormous value in life lived, no matter what place, no matter what color, no matter what gender, no matter what sexual choice. And I think he/she must do that with the highest level of craft mastery.

Okoro: How about space and time? As a writer, do you assign yourself a particular schedule for your writing? For instance, how many books you have to publish within a year.

Plumpp: No. I try to express what I need to express. And it does not matter how long it takes. And it does not matter how many books. I try to express a vision, and I have no idea of how that is calibrated in terms of books.

Okoro: I once heard you say you write for a wide audience. Can you explain what you mean?

Plumpp: What I mean is, I am very much aware of the great canonic text of Western literature and I think that they are fairly a model. So I'm trying to master the craft of writing outside the style, if I can satisfy myself that I've done the best I could. That's how you take that statement. I'm not satisfied simply if I won some accolades.

Okoro: Do you write with any kind of audience in mind?

Plumpp: I write from the depth of my being. And I'm glad if anyone out there shares my vision.

Okoro: Would you consider your writing social commentary? For instance, on page 58 of *Velvet BeBop Kente Cloth*, you touch on some serious issues often identified with American culture.

Plumpp: Is it social commentary? It is social commentary, but not simply social commentary. It is not social commentary for the sake of social commentary. I think that within the discourse, the call for discourse, the individualizing of the call for discourse often attributes the writer's real role. But I'm not even a part of this yet.

Okoro: Who is Sterling D. Plumpp?

Plumpp: Sterling D. Plumpp is an individual whose ancestor is African, whose poetry style is from the great literary traditions of Western literature, and who has different routes of analyzing collection through West African poetry and form as handed down through the poems of the Negro spirituals, the African Xhosa poems, the blues, and probably, socially, lastly, the jazz which originated with how the Africans played the drum. So I am kind of a hybrid individual who cannot claim to be solely African. And neither can I claim to be solely European. I am blessed with the Christian vision of life that is modified by the cultural survivals of traditional African life as expressed in the ways of worship at black churches.

Okoro: How important is landscape to your writing?

Plumpp: I was born in 1940 on a plantation outside of the town of Clinton in Mississippi, to be exact. Therefore, when I was trying to discover my voice, I visited the place where I was born. So I was born in Clinton, but my literary voice was born under the harsh conditions of Chicago. And the attempt to utilize jazz and blues comes from my attempt to recognize Chicago as a place where I was born as an artist, and South Africa and Africa because of the geographical theme in that it is one of the few places where I have experienced homecoming both physically and spiritually at the same time, because of similar conditions particular in South Africa, because of Africans living in the rural area, establishing ethnic enclaves in cities where they maintain cultural continuity, going out of the mines, and moving from the land and coming to the factories of the north. So landscape is very important to me, geographically and thematically.

Okoro: Let us go back to *Velvet BeBop Kente Cloth*. What inspired the writing?

Plumpp: First and foremost, I've written about jazz in two books. I've written about blues in *Blues: The Story Always Untold* and in *Johannesburg and Other Poems*. I've written about jazz in *Horn Man* and in *Ornate with Smoke*. So, as a prequel to the second half of the twentieth century in America, I sequenced these parts; I am drawing to rest my affair with Bird (Charlie Parker). I had to visit bebop, and I had to visit the kind of mastery of virtuosity that equips the tool that they are using. Now, there is a precedent that led directly to me picking a piano. The Association for the Advancement of Creative Musicians was one. This reminds me of an interview Miles and Bird had with a gentleman. The man asked Bird if he was surprised that he invented bebop. Bird said no. Later during the interview, he said for twenty-five years before he invented bebop, he practiced eleven to fourteen hours a day (Laughs). So that just blew me away. You know what I mean. It takes bebop style to another level. Then the other experience I can recall was when I was speaking with Fred Anderson who was seventy years old at the time. I asked him how often he practiced a day. He said, "O men, when I used to work a lot, I used to practice eight hours a day." I said, "Fred, I am talking about daily." He said, "Men, I don't have no time to practice daily. I only practice three or four hours." I think this tells you something about this great music called jazz. If you had a lot of genius, then you had extreme dedication.

Okoro: In your introduction to *Velvet BeBop Kente Cloth*, you took an introspective journey on the foundation of black music in America. Please elaborate on that point.

Plumpp: I think that whether one is huge, or whether one is talking about the business of the craft, the acquisition of one language leads to the development of another one. Because to the extent that you don't have a language to express your own humanity, your own desires, your own feelings, and to convey that to others, I think that you'll have to set it up by the pattern of forms. I don't think that African Americans do that. I think that they invented a language. And this language allowed them to erect a wealth of songs on the skeletons of their precedent, which allows them to elaborate themselves.

Okoro: How important is bebop to the arts and the individual then?

Plumpp: I think when one thinks of Max Roach, Reverend Brown, Art Blakely, you are seeing incredible virtuoso of mastery of bebop individuality. Each one of them is a drum, and each one of them is his own individual act. And likewise, if you go to Bird's house or Thelonious Monk, or Fred, you are looking at mastery, or, in light of all, mastery of the piano. So that for all custody is personalized. You look at Lester Young and Charlie Parker, among others, and you reconcile their own individual acts. I think that you are looking at individual art too.

Okoro: In what way would you consider yourself as someone who chronicles history through writing?

Plumpp: I consider myself as someone who chronicles the saga of Africans as it has been spread out through the diaspora. I chronicle that symbolically.

Okoro: I realize that name-calling remains pivotal to your poetry. Is this style something you adopted from an early influence or is it another Plumpp construction?

Plumpp: I've read a number of South African Xhosa poets in translation. I felt it was necessary for me to conjure the experience of the African artists, to Bop them into a system meaningful to my vision. That is one level. At the other level, I thought that one of the personal deters of human beings is to enlighten forms, or give others names. I thought that that was a form of writing the poem.

Okoro: Thanks for the clarification. Which writer(s) do you consider important to your understanding of serious literature?

Plumpp: In many parts, it'll be Amiri Baraka. Because I thought in many ways he imposes the model improvisation with the vernacular. He did miraculously with *Twenty Volume Suicide Note, Dead Lecturer, Black Magic, Dutchman, Slave, System of Dante's Hell,* and *Blues People.* I mean, it is an enormous achievement. Another writer is Larry Neal, because of his penetrating essays threading the black aesthetic rather than appealing to a black audience. His brilliant mastery of form is also worth mentioning. The other one is Dennis Brutus. *Letters to Martha,* I think, brilliantly shows this genre of political-imprisoned voice. The other one would be the poet Aimé Césaire. The crafting of his work and the camaraderie idea is very telling. I understand he is an underpaid poet who did major work within sixty to seventy years. Also, the poets Nikki Giovanni and Sonia Sanchez are very important names in this regard. Their collective contributions, be it as crafters of forms, or their experimentation with the haiku, without a doubt, is evidence of the value of their body of work.

Okoro: What do you see yourself doing when academic life demands a break?

Plumpp: I think I'll take a year away from teaching. Teaching is one way to confront people with the problems that you face. And I think it is the most direct way of confronting or settling problems that you are faced with on one level. Also, it is a fascinating way to reflect on how one has evolved over the years as a writer.

Okoro: What is next for you as a writer?

Plumpp: Although I have written a lot of poetry at this particular time, I think I have to begin to assemble works, which I might publish as an anthology of my works.

Okoro: How do you wish readers would remember Sterling Plumpp when it is all said and done with writing?

Plumpp: It is simple. That I am a writer who tries to live my life to its fullest, that I am a writer who is cognizant that I have the long concern for longevity, that I am a writer who lived the best I could, and that I'll not make a big deal about my living. And I hope no one will make a big deal about my death.

On Transmissions and Translations: Blues and the Poetry of Sterling D. Plumpp

Michael Antonucci and John Edgar Wideman / 2009

From *Valley Voices: A Literary Review* 9.1 (Spring 2009): 123–30. Reprinted by permission of *Valley Voices: A Literary Review*.

John Edgar Wideman spoke with me on January 19, 2009, about Sterling Plumpp, poetry, and the blues impulse(s) in black letters. Professor Wideman's admiration and affection for Professor Plumpp was made evident throughout our telephone conversation. The energy Professor Wideman brought to the discussion that follows is an example of what he calls an "acte gratuit."

Michael Antonucci: In the "Afterword" of Sterling Plumpp's *Blues Narratives* (1999), you write about the omnipresence of blues within Sterling's work. You describe his poetry as "a philosophic inquiry about blues as world view, as consolation and rumination, long quarrel and reconciliation with godhead, blues as path for coming to terms with existence." Could you discuss your understanding of blues functioning as an expressive mode and its approaching this kind of multivalent omnipresence?

John Edgar Wideman: The quote, which I recognize, is one I certainly believed when I spoke it, as I believe it now. But one's words coming back at one's self always do have a strange ring: a sort of intimidating ring because in certain occasions spirit moves, at least I'm moved by the spirit, and the spirit takes over and I speak both for myself and for whatever sort of forces there are beyond me, which sometimes channel through me. I don't want that to sound mysterious, but for me the blues is extraordinarily mysterious and the ability to express some of the complexity and some of the range of blues is the same as expressing the range and the intimacy and the power of a life.

The blues is an idiom and we can identify certain historical facts about places where it originated, various steps in its development. We can build up that sort of dossier of the blues. But at the same time, I think it's much more a kind of timeless and placeless phenomenon. That is to say we are born and from the very moment we open our eyes, we begin to try to make sense of things; we see and hear and begin to smell things and we have the sense of other people around us, if we're lucky. From that wild and absolutely untamable, incomprehensible state, we mix and begin to form an identity and those idioms those facts of life—like being born in West Africa or the instruments that play the music of the particular place [where] you live, the other kind of people that migrate and move into areas that you do—all those innumerable, incalculable forces begin to give you a certain way of being in the world. And that way, that mode, is essentially who you are and who you will always be. And it's imprinted at a very early age, differentiated by culture differentiated by various circumstances and conditions, yet we all share many qualities. In these modes of being and shared qualities, that's where the blues begins to take shape.

So, to cut back through the arc of a life and the arc of an individual life like mine or yours or Sterling's is, in theory, a process that would have taken into account that kind of complexity and that kind of range of how we come into the world and what we do when we get here. These are the roots of the blues. The rest is detail. Somehow that early imprint stays with us or becomes distinctive enough that it's recognizable and it distinguishes people and the same way that the manner of speaking the particular language one learns to speak is stamped by the very earliest experiences, complex conscious and unconscious experiences of beginning of being.

I can't break it down any simpler than that and I realize I'm not saying anything simple; I may be saying something a little confused or maybe someday I'm not quite understanding myself, but I do know that one has to start with that sort of breadth and that sort of humility and, at the same time, attempt for vast outreach to begin to explain or, not to explain, but to talk about the blues idiom and why it's so important, why it can structure poetry, why it can structure love affairs, why it can structure the way a woman would try to console her child, the way a preacher would attempt to console a congregation, the way slaves talk to one another when they weren't allowed to talk and really didn't even speak one another's languages; there were tonalities, there were rhythms, there was a vocabulary that was shared that went back to the roots that I just very peremptorily, I guess, tried to describe.

MA: When you talk about breadth, humility, and vast outreach, that touches upon something I see going on in the way Sterling Plumpp incorporates the blues in his work. When Martin Scorsese contacted you about contributing to the volume that became the companion to the PBS series on the blues, you chose to write about Sterling's work. Could you say more about this decision? You could have written about anyone for this but his work or what you see in his work became your template for discussing the blues.

JEW: My friendship and my experiences with Sterling influenced this decision. He is a certain kind of man. In so many things that he does—the way he speaks, the way he walks, the way he treats people—he represents continuities that seem to me extremely familiar and I can't always locate in words those continuities. I don't have the knowledge; I don't know Sterling enough to be able to rattle off major incidents in his life or his friends or his anecdotes about his family. But, the way that he relates, the way that I know that I can ask him certain questions, that I can trust him with the answers to certain questions he asks me, all that suggests a kind of almost preternatural sharing and it's really not anything that I guess, if you were smart enough and around him enough you could probably, to some extent, explain it.

I suppose it's like art: you can never explain a particular work of art no matter how much information you gather about it. You can't explain a person no matter how many facts you organize, but there is a push, a *je ne c'est quoi*, that makes the work what it is. And Sterling, as a person, makes available to me just who he is in the truest sense, and that's a rare quality; he has been that way from the first time I met him. It's a gift and I appreciate it in his verse, the way he drinks and offers me a drink. There's just that accessibility and that sense that we're on the same track.

MA: In her essay "Blues Roots of Contemporary Afro-American Poetry" (1979), Sherley Anne Williams writes, "Blues is essentially an oral form meant to be heard rather than read, and the techniques and structures used to such powerful purpose in the songs cannot always be transferred directly to literary traditions within which, by definition, that Afro-American poets write." If you would, discuss any technical or structural tensions that you see when considering blues-oriented literary expression. Are there particular ways that, for instance, poetry succeeds in translating blues to the written page? Or fiction? If so, could you speak to how or where you see that dynamic taking place in another writer's work, where it succeeds, maybe even in your own work.

JEW: I will tackle that question about transmission or translation—as I think it's a question about both those things—in as concrete a way as I can. Just take the aspect of repetition. Blues lyrics, as I understand it, the blues musical line, depends and is structured on repetition. In an oral form, each repetition can be nuanced or varied. When you write, "my girl done gone and left me," then sing "my girl done gone and left me," it's the same words in both cases. They are repeated, but there's a variation in terms of words, in terms of what we can transcribe. You can play around with the lyrics, you can play around with the spelling, you can use dashes, you can use capital letters, you can print some of the letters, that phrase, in red, sometimes in blue, and that just becomes a kind of a different game that doesn't neces- sarily get any closer to the written page script to the true sense of variation that's embodied in the voice and the alternation of voice and some instru- ment, guitar, whatever. So, we're talking about comparing literary text with an actual performance of a blues. The same issues are raised in this as are raised by any transmission of oral to written [forms]. You have to invent and stylize a written form to capture repetition in the same sense that the artist stylizes and invents the oral repetitions.

Now how to do that and how you can do that and who has done it well, those are other questions, but that is the issue always. Nothing is given. Translation of a poem is always a challenge to write another poem. Books repeat themselves in one sense. The words on the page stay the same, but the readers are different and so readers put different inflection, different meaning into words. And two different readers reading the same words. How does a writer take that into account? To me this becomes a question of creativity. It's a question of not taking anything for granted and understand- ing the deep structure of the idiom that you are attempting to work into an artistic form. And these questions are written about, I don't think, not a lot, in terms of the blues. So I'm just touching on one aspect which I would hope might be suggestive to people and a place to begin. What about repeti- tion? What does repetition mean in literate versus oral forms?

MA: When you talk about books repeating themselves you almost seem to suggest that there's a blues reading—or way of engaging what's on the page. It seems that you're imagining an interaction with a text that main- tains "blues nuances" and even non-blues rooted texts might be "blues'd" or translated, if you would, into the blues. Is this the kind of dynamic you see emerging from translation challenge that you just raised?

JEW: I heard Quincy Troupe read Achebe's *Things Fall Apart* once. He read a conversation between the two characters that occurs early in the book, Okonkwo's father and another man, whose name escapes me at the moment, a villager who was a musician. The musician is kind of a ne'er do well; Okonkwo, of course, is very ambitious and very dynamic and wants to embody, and in a sense does embody, all the great traditions of the Igbo culture and Igbo manhood. And so they're, in one sense, not very equal. One is the type of man that the society wants to produce and the other is the type of man that the society would seem to want to forget. The point is when I read that, I got a lot out of it and it meant something to me, but then when I heard Quincy read it, it became a blues dialogue, a blues conversation and his rendering was all timing and inflection and emphasis, pauses, but he brought to it a kind of blues sensibility that was quite striking. So, yes, could one read Chairman Mao's *Red Book* with blues intonation? Maybe.

MA: In this light, I think it would be interesting to hear your thoughts considering the blues in Sterling's poetry as a "mode of discovery." Specifically, I'm drawing again from your afterword in *Blues Narratives* and I'm also thinking about Sterling's *Velvet BeBop Kente Cloth* (2003). In particular, I'm recalling your statement, "Whether in Mississippi or Capetown the poet knows exactly who he is, writes with profound certainty of his roots. . . . So you don't get the sense the poet knows what's coming next. . . . The mode is discovery."

JEW: One of the delights of any art is how it reverberates or how the rhythms of that art work, whether they're visual, auditory, a combination. How they present the familiar and the unexpected and how those two seemingly different qualities are mixed and how in the really best work, after a while you don't know the difference; you can't distinguish the difference. In other words, time is engaged in a way that is very like the way we, in a very raw and primitive sense, engage time every day in our own lives. That is to say, there is sometimes a numbing sort of sameness and predictability, but yet we stay tuned because we never exactly know what's going to come next. And we, in fact, do not know what's going to come next no matter on how many occasions we've been to a particular sort of moment or job or kiss or pain; it can change in a minute, on a dime. And I think that's what the blues does with its themes and variations.

I think that's how Sterling understands the world; that it is a given; that we have no choice, but to regularize the rhythms of work, or the rhythms of lovemaking or the rhythms of singing. We have no choice, but to regularize ourselves, our voices, our bodies, to fit what we've seen before, what we've learned firsthand or what somebody's told us. And so we're always getting ready for that next moment; but there has to be something you leave out, some unexpressed thing left out that can account for or accommodate the moment that's stunning; stunning because it's good; stunning because it's bad; or the moment it doesn't even seem to come, or one that comes from such an odd place in a strange place we're not even sure where we were before and maybe everything has to start all over again. And that's the attitude that is brought to music by the blues.

MA: This pattern seems to be what Sterling's work examines throughout *Velvet BeBop Kente Cloth*, this profound sense of dislocation.
JEW: Well, dislocation is almost a contradiction in terms. Because how can you be dislocated but also be right there at the same time? And that's one of those paradoxes; one of those internal contradictions that is in a flatted note, or blue note, and this is something the music epitomizes taken in terms of larger structures as well, and larger attitudes. Sterling understands this and brings it into his work. But in terms of philosophy, or what one might call a philosophy, this constitutes a kind of reminiscence or imagining of what it means to live in a blues saturated being, personal being and universe.

MA: When I hear you saying this I can't help but hear Jim Trueblood. I hear him describing the predicament of being, knowing he needed to move but recognizing that he really could not; it sounds like you're describing those impossible positions where an individual could and couldn't; where he must but can't. This sort of collapsing of contradictions, something that Ellison understands, might have roots in the folk culture and is a phenomenon that is not unfamiliar to what Sterling calls a "peasant" background.
JEW: No matter who we think we are, in a sense, "*You ain't seen nothin' yet.*" And because we come into situations where our repertoire of response is inadequate and outmoded instantly. In these situations we have to be somebody else, we have to act in a way we've never acted before. Or, in fact, in retrospect as in the case of Trueblood, we are trying to make sense of the way we acted which we wouldn't have anticipated or goes against all the rules of who we thought we were. So, there's that kind of dislocation again.

And to what degree do we have tools, as human beings, to make sense of it and music is one way we try to make sense of it and music with lyrics particularly. That's the kind I understand more than any other kind. I think it lends itself to analysis in an interesting way because it is the combination of word and sound. But it's that sense of trying to be a person and believing it and making your best effort, but knowing that you can lose that protection that you spent so much time building up.

I remember the first time at Howard University my first college teaching class, the very first day; it was summer school, back in the '60s, I guess. I was home from Oxford, so it had to be like 1966, and I was at Howard teaching a summer school class. I had put on my three-piece suit in spite of the fact that it was hot and in those days teaching and being a professor was much more formal than it is now, so I was dressed to the nines. I was clean. I was ready. I'm standing at the door to introduce the students and I really had to be on my p's and q's because I was just a kid myself, not much older than the students and some of them were older than me because it was summer school. But anyway, there I am with my smile, but not too much of a smile, just kind of laid back and together and then I hear a voice: "John Wideman, what are you doing here?" And I saw somebody, a young lady I knew quite well and she's walking into the classroom and so there went my whole bag; there went my three-piece suit; there went my attitude and suddenly, I'm reeling, and not just because I'm necessarily compromised, which I was, by my relationship with that young lady, but it was the whole class, it was what are you going to teach? What is this African American stuff you're bringing to these students? Who are you and who are they and what is this game of separation that you're starting, that's your initial premise? So, it's funny, I'm learning, but I have to be prepared and strike out in a different direction.

MA: In the *Blues Narratives* "Afterword" you talk about "bardic I" in Plumpp's verse and discuss his profound personal experience and its impact on his individualized insights concerning a collective sense of being and identity. Michael S. Harper describes this blues impulse as "the I becoming the we." Can you speak to this movement from that singular to the plural, from the individual to the collective and how they inform this sort of "blues moments"?

JEW: There is a built-in change or there are built-in changes that have become quite traditional and I guess what both of us are calling a blues aesthetic and those changes are constituted by the things I've been talking about as I reflect on Sterling's poetry. And I think this comes in his way of saying and expressing the collective voices and a blues way of making distinctions: "I been doing this; he been doing that. Don't y'all hear me? Where y'all been tonight?" All of this part of the same song, running the grammatical changes of person and tense. And all of these combine to give this sort of texture and unpredictable context which I've spoken of before and others have, about great time. Well, I also think there's such a thing as "great grammar" where the voice is finding its own way to express itself using the categories of classical and conventional grammar, but breaking those and finding new ones and using combinations. That's why the word vernacular is so appropriate for the blues because it is language formation; language destabilization and building a new language, forms and modes and structures.

MA: That certainly can be applied to Sterling's poetics. It's evident in what he's doing right now with those line breaks that he works with and the slashes that he uses to score his poetry.

JEW: I've been working on a number of different projects of late, but one thing that I've been working on has taken me to Pound manuscripts and that certainly Sterling comes to this practice by way of a very strong tradition in American poetry from Walt Whitman on. Certainly, Emily Dickinson is trying to score the words on the page and it's to catch the illusiveness of speech and locate concrete structures that elude conventional grammar, conventional formatting on the page. So, this impulse is very American. I think I'll stop right there because it suggests where we need to go and that is you can't talk about America without talking about the blues and you can't talk about the blues without talking about America.

MA: You've written about "the generosity of the blues and the desire to show gratitude and to share in it." While you spoke this sensibility earlier, I am going to ask if you might comment further because many do not immediately associate or connect blues with the spirit of reciprocity. I can ground this by asking you if it's fair to describe blues and blues practitioners like Sterling as a conduit for "exchange"; maybe this gets back to the translation issue but it seems to connect well with the idea that difficulty in examining America without talking about or examining the blues.

JEW: I like to think that art, any type of artistic expression, is a gift from the artist to the audience and of course the audience has the option of returning the gift of attention, but I don't write—and I don't think Sterling does either—because I have any idea of what's going to come back or any idea that anything will come back at all. The impulse is to give; the impulse is to join in that chorus of voices, of words, that we respect so much that has given us an opportunity and a chance to practice the art that we practice; the ancestors, so to speak. We've been so impressed by them that we have no choice but to both respond to them and try to give what we've received from them, from those other voices. And the art is, in that sense, generous—the French would say an "*acte gratuit*"; you don't expect anything in exchange. It is a kind of pure giving. And what the blues singer does or what the troubadour did, is bring the news, bring the food—the spiritual food, intellectual food—and sometimes people paid him, sometimes people chased him off, sometimes he got brought into the community, sometimes somebody wanted to cut his throat for messing with his woman. Either way, it didn't matter; in this role you are a bearer of something that you love and respect and you want to share it and this overarching desire finds a way to get that message out there, to keep it alive and to keep yourself alive by doing so.

MA: This impulse is clearly something that I can say connects your work to Sterling's work. It's a privilege to have been able to talk with you. Thanks so much, Professor Wideman.
JEW: You're welcome and good luck with what you're doing.

(Special thanks to Betsy Rhode of Keene State College for her assistance in making this interview transcription possible.)

Sterling Plumpp Interview

Hermine Pinson / 2009

From Valley Voices: A Literary Review 9.1 (Spring 2009): 79–81. Reprinted by permission of *Valley Voices: A Literary Review.*

The interview was conducted with the poet between April 3 and April 6, 2009, in writing and over the telephone.

Hermine Pinson: You have been asked many times about the blues and jazz as inextricable to your poetry, but how about other musical genres? How do they inform your work?

Sterling Plumpp: When I suggest how blues and jazz inform my work, I'm talking about the music and musicality of African American culture. Gospel music informs my work, Negro sermon has informed my work, rhythmic prayer styles have informed my work, doo wop has influenced my work, R&B, as well as diaspora music from the Caribbean and South America.

I inherited the folk culture. The moan and the deep moan, that was in church. But when I went to Catholic school, with these literate black people I was slowly through the back door introduced to literacy. You cannot give back your literacy.

HP: *Black Rituals* was the first and only book of essays you ever wrote. What prompted you to write this cultural critique of black modern life, especially life in the South?

SP: Part of my perception of the Black Arts Movement is that the definitions and perceptions were of urban life, and if I had a critique it would have to be from the place of my origins, which was the Deep South.

HP: You have credited poets and writers such as Haki Madhubuti and Keorapetse Kgositsile, and Amiri Baraka with having a significant influence on your early work.

SP: The central things that I took from these three outstanding poets are their commitments to having an important message in their poetry, as well as their superior usage of a honed vernacular from black music and black speech.

HP: How did your immigration to the Midwest affect your perspective? Was the move partially responsible for your focus on geography in your work?

SP: The immigration from Mississippi to Chicago complicated my view of myself and complicated my view of African American culture and African American life. Therefore, I began to view blues-inspired poems as much more related to jazz rhythms and structure than to black folk blues poems.

HP: Is the election of Barack Obama to the presidency an indication of progress, in light of the goals of the civil rights movement?

SP: Yes, it is an indication of progress, as well as the emergence of Bill Cosby, Oprah Winfrey, Michael Jordan, Tiger Woods, and a host of superiorly educated, doctorally trained African Americans from top flight universities over the last four decades.

HP: What younger poets do you see as having promise in the literary world?

SP: I know the work of Tyehimba Jess as well as a host of Cave Canem poets.

HP: What is the role of the poet in the twenty-first century? What is his/her responsibility? Does the poet speak for the people?

SP: The poet's responsibility in the twenty-first century is to defend and exude individuality. If the poet speaks the truth about his or her experience, the poet speaks for the people.

HP: You may be the first and only poet in history to win the lottery. How has the lottery affected your life, if at all?

SP: The lottery granted me a small amount of means so I do not have to worry. It also sharpened my understanding of how most Americans lack funds and means.

HP: What misconceptions about your work would you correct? Put another way, what do you think scholars and critics have missed or gotten wrong in their consideration of your work?

SP: If they have read my work and are aware that I am a poet who has undergone an extensive metamorphosis, then there are no misconceptions.

HP: *Blues Narratives* is projected as part of an epic work, *Mfua's Song*. Could you explain the title and plan of the upcoming work and how it relates to your past volumes?

SP: Mfua is the name I gave to the mother of the oldest known relative in the family, Tympe, who I am told was born in 1772 and died in 1903. I am sure she was from West Africa and for some reason I thought Tympe's mother would be Mfua. The long work, *Mfua's Song*, is based upon my entire family's ancestry. It is the oral telling, not the examination of records. I plan to write the epic history of Mfua's descendants down to the twentieth century.

HP: Are there questions this interview did not ask that you would like to address?

SP: Yes, who is Larry Neal? Larry Neal should be read for his brilliant poetry. (*Hoodoo Hollerin' Bebop Ghosts*) and for his outstanding essays discussing the task of fomenting a literary "Black Aesthetic." He is a genius who should live in the minds of successive generations and be read.

HP: In a past interview, the interviewer asked you about the authenticity of your name, Sterling Plumpp? Would you care to comment on this?

SP: My mother was unmarried at the time that I was born and her maiden name was Emmanuel, but my grandparents thought I should be given the name of my father. My father was Cyrus Plumpp.

An Interview with Sterling Plumpp

John Zheng / 2013

From *Journal of Ethnic American Literature* 3 (2013): 127–37. Reprinted by permission of *Journal of Ethnic American Literature*.

John Zheng: Professor Plumpp, you are a native son of Clinton, Mississippi. How has your coming of age in Mississippi influenced your poetry?
Sterling Plumpp: Several things: The rural agricultural black peasant life-style and experience nourished my body and soul. The families adjacent to the farm my grandfather sharecropped left me with an abundance of humanity to observe and participate in. But most importantly, my maternal grandfather, Victor Emmanuel, 1880–1955, exemplified a manhood I idol-ized. He had a fourth-grade education, seven children and a firm commit-ment to rule his house. He was sixty when I was born and a deacon in his church and a mason. His prayers on bended knee before he retired for the night and when he arose in the morning are, perhaps, the impetus for my love of blues and my interest in black vernacular. I was never weaned from my appreciation of how the peasant voice could celebrate and affirm life.

I never lived in Clinton proper; I lived in the country on a farm where people planted, chopped, cultivated, and picked cotton. They had gar-dens and killed game, raised chickens and hogs. They were a community of neighbors. They would sometimes send a child over to borrow a little baking powder, sugar, or lard. They attended the motley array of churches within a five-mile radius: Wells Grove, Mound Hood, St. Thomas, Pilgrim Rest, Holy Ghost, and Pleasant Green.

Here I heard tales from their lives and they resonated in me. When I read *Uncle Tom's Children* (Richard Wright), I learned a meaning of black-ness and self in Clinton. My books—*Clinton*, *Steps to Break the Circle*, *Blues Narratives*, *Home/Bass*, and *Black Rituals*—arise from my memory and appreciation of my emergence in Clinton.

JZ: I remember when we first met around ten years ago at the blues symposium in Jonesboro, Arkansas, you mentioned Richard Wright, saying he was your man. How did he influence you in writing?

SP: When I initially read *Black Boy* and *Uncle Tom's Children* in 1962, I had no idea how to incorporate personal experiences into the literary genres. Most importantly, I learned the value of reading a variety of genres and seeing the world through the eyes of authors I read. Finally I learned how the great capitalist nation with a constitution as a work-in-progress had harmed, dehumanized, and exploited many under ideology of both race and class. Wright taught me a method of patterning my experiences so that I could make aesthetic sense out of them.

JZ: I feel that your journey out of Mississippi was not at all a way to escape the hardships, but to travel for good education. What was your goal in each stop of your travel?

SP: When I graduated from high school at the age of twenty, education or the opportunity to acquire skills needed to fashion a life was utmost in my mind. I discovered Greek literature and the power of literacy before I discovered education. After I read *The Odyssey* and *Oedipus Rex*, my Roman Catholic and southern upbringing world was in shambles. I knew intuitively that those who mastered the word in great literary texts were the true saviors of bodies and souls.

True, Mississippi had been hardships, which eclipsed any possibility of my achieving selfhood there. But it was also a place within the small margins of school and church where I had compiled enough hope to propel me to dream. Therefore, my two years at St. Benedict's College in Atchison, Kansas, had exposed me to Western civilization and a greater sense of literacy so that my eventual move to Chicago was tolerable.

JZ: Any writing about your experience, insight, or discovery from your travel?

SP: Yes, *Johannesburg and Other Poems* reflects my insights gained from meeting people engaged in revolutionary struggle. I learned you find yourself involved in combat for state power; you do whatever is necessary to persevere or you perish. I heard gunshots and fleeting footsteps all night from my room in a Johannesburg hotel; therefore, I came away with the belief that the chronicle of revolution is what poet Mongane Serote calls "a tough tale."

JZ: With your early years of involvement in the Black Arts Movement in Chicago and with your publication of *Black Rituals*, do you consider yourself an intellectual of the Black Arts Movement?

SP: I consider myself a participant in the Black Arts Movement. I consider myself a poet who tries to steep himself in literacy. Also, I think the term Black Arts Movement has no meaning unless it is understood as a people's quest to implement Black power in their lives. There is a Black Nationalist tradition in African American history. And anthropologists have demonstrated and concluded that the millions of Africans captured, transported across the Atlantic, and enslaved in the "New World" improvised, developed, and maintained a culture that kept African survivals on continued aspects of their cultures from the continent.

I spent thirty years of my life seeking and developing structures in the university where the accurate assessments of African American life and experience were a reality. I am familiar with pertinent bibliography of the Black Arts Movement. I read *Black Liberator, Black Dialogue, Soul Book, Journal of Black Poetry, Negro Digest/Black World, Obsidian*, and *Callaloo*. I studied the anthologies, *For Malcolm* and *Black Fire* and was published by Third World Press, Broadside Press, *Negro Digest/Black World*, and *Journal of Black Poetry*. I am simply a poet looking into my entangled migrations.

JZ: For poetry and essay writing, for instance, *Blues Narratives* and *Black Rituals*, which one did you find most demanding in your writing?

SP: I found *Blues Narratives* most demanding and illusive for two reasons: (1) *Blues Narratives* is simply two sections from a much longer work-in-progress, *Mfua's Song*. The long poem is primary in familial voices across generations. When a professor friend of mine read the longer works, he said the two sections that became *Blues Narratives* seemed like a complete book. (2) *Black Rituals* (nonfiction), on the other hand, was my attempt to deal with southern roots and the importance of church and black people and their "rituals." Since poetry literally requires one to invent a language to write in, it was much harder for me.

JZ: Some people would say that blues is a healing. When you wrote *Blues Narratives*, did you feel it was a healing? If it was, what was it?

SP: When I wrote *Blues Narratives*, it was a healing because the two figures I created, my mother Mary (1920–1980) and my grandfather Victor (1880–1955), had been dead nineteen and forty-four years respectively. The crux of the burden of my soul was that I had not made an appropriate goodbye to either one. I am affecting a blues singer for Mary—the mother I had never bonded with. I felt her voice had been heard. And I finally had gathered a chance to stare at Victor's tale and not be destroyed. Yes, it was healing for me.

JZ: In fact, you wrote a poem titled "Healing Music," published in the 2009 special issue of *Valley Voices* on your poetry. At the end of the poem, you say, "He makes his music. / Lord / healing music for the soul." Anything interesting to say about the healing?

SP: Yes, I believe that the essence of logotherapy by Viktor Frankl is that the individual stares that which threatens his or her existence in the face. The individual learns to do this in order to get rid of its threat.

JZ: What inspired you to write poetry? During your early years of writing, who was or were your greatest inspiration(s)?

SP: I don't exactly know but several writer examples come to mind. I always knocked off my feet by the manner in which LeRoi Jones springs metaphors and imagery from unsuspecting corners in *Preface to a Twenty Volume Suicide Note* and *The Dead Lecturer*. I have always envied Gwen Brooks for her love affair with language and the people in *A Street in Bronzeville* and *In the Mecca*. Finally the majesty of elocution Sterling Brown brings to reading his poems—he is a master.

JZ: When you are in a Chicago jazz club listening to the jazz horn and rhythm, do you have a feeling that your writing comes along with the music?

SP: I have a feeling that I am hearing a poetic language that does not yet exist. I scribble notes and try to affect lines that aspire to genius and eloquence I just heard.

JZ: You are a bluesjazz poet. Could you say something to help a reader to better understand your bluesjazz poetry?

SP: My bluesjazz poetry is one writer's attempt or quest to find language that owes a debt to the brilliance of black diasporic music.

JZ: I believe when you wrote blues poetry, you had to think in blues, listen in blues and imagine in blues and let blues occupy your body and soul. Could you give us a taste of your creative thinking about blues?

SP: The most remarkable discovery I have made poetically is that I am not a folk poet, I come from rural roots in an all-black environment but somehow literacy affords me an additional prism through which to view the world and life. I had wanted or intended Muddy Waters's vernacular, but somehow bebop inventions kept getting in my way.

I accept the challenge of diasporic cultural legacy with the realization that literacy imparts on me the necessity to always invent and reinvent what I think I hear. That is really how I began using slashes. I thought I was hearing two different language possibilities in phrases and I wanted a pause longer than a comma but not yet as abrupt and definite stop as a period. I accept the validity of the folk voice while simultaneously realizing that literacy requires me to do something original or improvisational or unique in what I hear.

Folk expressions are artistic launching pads for my imagination, and I am a poet who hears language rather than thinks it. My process in blues poetry is to hear it and figure out how to procure a poetic language for it. I long not to go beyond blues but to sketch or exhaust blues possibility in poetic lines, phrases, or metaphor.

JZ: What's the difference between Delta blues and Chicago blues?
SP: Delta Blues is more folk blues without the sophisticated rhythmic dialogue between bass and drum. An example of Delta blues is "My Home Is in the Delta" by Muddy Waters, and his "Hoochie Coochie Man" is an example of Chicago blues.

JZ: Howard Reich writes in the *Chicago Tribune* that you are a poet laureate of Chicago jazz and blues, a man who conveys in words as much melody and rhythm as the musicians he immortalizes in print. Could you use a poem of yours to explain about this melodious and rhythmic conveyance?
SP: "My Name" from *Home/Bass* illustrates melodious and rhythmic conveyance. The lines:

Where /I
revoke/echoes
from/silences.
I/heard
my daddy
surrender.

are blues lyrics and melody and the lines:

> All
> my/talk.
> A/song.
> All
> my/conversation.
> A/song.

continue my melody. The slashes emphasize the pauses one sometimes hears in blues singers' styles.

> In
> side/my eyes.
> A/miniature
> burial/ground.
> I/survey.
> two/white
> horses. Mud/as high
> way. This/is
> my father's/story.
> I/sing. This/is
> my grand
> father's/story.
>
> I/sing.

The above is also a blues melody, but not in the blues form. Writing poetry too much in blues form is cliché because it is too redundant, too repetitive. It is difficult for the writer to utilize or affect a personal original voice in it.

JZ: I like the picture of Fred Anderson published in *Valley Voices*, a literary review that I have edited for thirteen years. Looking at it, you can feel the swing and sway of his horn. Did his music influence your writing?

SP: Von Freeman, tenor saxophonist, and Fred Anderson, tenor saxophonist, influenced my work a great deal. They influenced the manner in which I heard language and strove to create lines. Fred would dialogue with me in various narratives regarding jazz musicians. I always thought the most original and penetrating music I heard was bebop. In the early 1960s, I had witnessed Sonny Stitt play a half dozen times or so. His unstated mastery of the alto sax forced me to imagine how Bird arrived at bebop language. Von Freeman was a consummate bebopper and Fred Anderson was equally original and innovative. He lived to know and explore his horn. I learned to try and do the same with my pen on the page.

JZ: Could you use a poem of yours to illustrate the swing and sway of music you tried to convey?
SP: "Eight" from *Velvet BeBop Kente Cloth*:

In the/Beginning
was/Nothing
and/God made some
thing/Out of no
thing/And Bird riff Be
Bop out/Of nothing.

Creation/Hold deeds
to/Nothing.

In America/More folks killed
for/Nothing than for some
thing/Cats say Bird
had a/Pocket
dictionary/Of nothing
He/Carry round.

Fred say/I carry
round/A library
of/Nothing.
I/Reed every word every
day/I rite my name
in/Axe depictions.

Dizzy once/Say.
He/A UFO controller
of Bop/He riff
directions/In nothing.

The poem, "Eight," illustrates my interpretation in language of how a bebopper's language might swing and sway to convey his music and message.

JZ: Any interesting episodes about your friendship with Fred Anderson and about Velvet Lounge?

SP: My most solemn observation is that Fred Anderson was proprietor of the Velvet Lounge and those brilliant musicians who performed there regularly had deeds to the velvet space where performances were held.

JZ: What do you expect a reader to get from your poetry? Experience, history, or poetic style?

SP: I expect the reader to view me as a proud American who descended from Africans, who, despite enslavement, produced, improvised, and maintained a unique musical culture. I want my poetry to allude to the history and experience of the creators of that musical culture.

JZ: What would be your personal favorite among your poems?

SP: It's hard to have a favorite among poems, but the text of *Blues Narratives* is definitely the most meaningful to me. It allowed me to converse with a mother I never bonded with and allowed me to appreciate how much a grandfather had given me.

JZ: Could you say something about the use of slashes in your poetry? What's the important function of using slashes and how do you expect a reader to understand them?

SP: What I will say about "slashes" and their use in my poetry is that I began using them in my notes when I tried to write about Von Freeman and Fred Anderson. I told the editor at Third World Press, if they were a problem for readers, to eliminate them. While influenced by jazz, bebop in particular, I began hearing things in language and I needed a pause longer than a comma, but not as definite as a period. The "slashes" taught me to hear and seek to hear different meanings in ordinary language. They forced me to play, in my way, with language sometimes for the sake of playing with the sound of it.

JZ: Reginald Gibbons says in his introduction to your most recent poetry book, *Home/Bass*, that you are "as sophisticated in the way [you take] our language apart as is any avant-gardist." How do you treat language in your poetry? Could you give us an example about using the language to convey your meaning?

SP: Blues lyrics and references to particular blues singers' styles are sources and inspiration for my language. Therefore, I might write:

> I got him with
>   a/Bessie Smith
>   & Wesson lyric
>   fired at/close range

This utilizing double entendre or weaponizing and the sheer power of blues lyric as delivered by a master are things I try to allude to.

JZ: Finally, any new writing project underway?

SP: Yes, I am completing a memoir about a Mississippi peasant who migrates from one geography to another, who has something in his ears he cannot forget: the lessons from songs, prayers, and sermons imbedded in the tones of my grandparents born in 1880 and 1890 respectively.

Poet of the Ear: An Interview with Sterling D. Plumpp

James Ballowe / 2014

From *Fifth Wednesday Journal* 14 (Spring 2014): 10–18. Reprinted by permission of *Fifth Wednesday Journal*.

This interview with Sterling Plumpp took place on the morning of January 14, 2014, in a Downers Grove, Illinois Public Library conference room not much larger than a carrel. The formal interview lasted a little over an hour. But the discussion continued well into the afternoon. Now into his eighth decade, Sterling continues to evoke the life and work of those in whose world he feels fortunate to have lived.

Fifth Wednesday Journal: Sterling, Howard Reich begins a review of *Home/Bass*, your latest collection published in 2013, by declaring, "[Plumpp] is the poet laureate of Chicago jazz and blues, a man who conveys in words as much melody and rhythm as the musicians he immortalizes in print."

That accolade from a distinguished critic of jazz, blues, bebop, and gospel at the *Chicago Tribune* begs putting your work into the perspectives of a lifetime in which you have honed a form and a language that gives shape and voice to your own cultural and intellectual experiences. To help understand that background readers might want to look up an interview Reginald Gibbons did with you in 2003, published in full in the April 27, 2010, issue of the on-line *TriQuarterly*. The interview produced a remarkable memoir in which you describe your personal journey from Clinton, Mississippi, where you grew up in the forties to Chicago and from a childhood on a tenant farm to a career as a professor at the University of Illinois at Chicago and as a chronicler in poetry of a family and musical history which you have consistently evoked over the years.

Could you begin by commenting on how these new poems in *FWJ* continue the work you have been doing?

Sterling Plumpp: Yes. When I began writing poetry in the 1960s there were three individuals who made an imprint on my mind: Ralph Ellison, James Baldwin, and LeRoi Jones [later Amiri Baraka], the latter mainly because of his book *Blues People*. And initially what I thought I was writing in terms of black poetry was then black musical poetry and culture. Ralph Ellison, more so than any other American writer, felt that the Negro spiritual, blues, and jazz perhaps rivaled anything produced by the world in the last four or five hundred years. And that led me to try to understand the craft side of it, initially from the spoken word from blues, then through sophisticated bebop.

There are things that happen in bebop. And that is that jazz is deconstructed from big bands down to a combo, a trio, and you could begin to focus on one instrument with a great rhythm section. And what captured my mind so much in that, the man who is credited with co-inventing it, Charlie Parker, was not a composer. So [laughing] how do you arrive at that kind of musical plan? I spent a great deal of time watching people listening to Sonny Stitt. He was a great bebopper.

And what happened by the time I wrote "Migration"—what happens when you grow up as a tenant farmer—is that the vernacular becomes your first language. It takes you a long time to understand that, so much so that first time I heard the blues, I was intrigued by it because it sounded like my grandparents sounded when they would pray aloud together every night before they went to bed and when they got up in the morning. That was the sound I mean rhythmically, more important as they were talking to the Heavenly Father. I did not understand it at the time, and so I'm drawn to it. And years later when I would see—in particular Muddy Waters who had taken devices that come from preachers' prayers and then put into blues— they were singing, and what's going through my imagination is that in the process of developing Negro spirituals and later blues and jazz, the African American was creating the basis for a new language.

And the problem is that I'm a poet. And what happened was that I had been to private school, I had been to college and university, and I had to tell myself that I was not Muddy Waters. [laughter] "You're not folk, boy; you read all these books." And the questions is, "What happens when you add literacy to all that experience?" That's what I'm thinking. I mean I'm not thinking about these models that come from music. The task is trying to find a language that evokes that. And fortunately for me I knew the family history of when and where and how the family had migrated from about 1938 down through 1960. And so I had the details of it. So one time I was writing the details, and when I wrote "Miles and Moles" I had to try to deal with—no matter what my beliefs are—the fact that these tenant farmers were people who believed in a God, who had a sense of morality, who had a sense of community, and I tried to bring that and tried to keep it real in the sense of the actual hardship and a sense of celebration. And the thing is I had come to know that they had found a kind of miniature heaven that did not last always. The fact that you could buy a bottle of wine or a new suit was a kind of heaven, and it did not last always.

FWJ: Like Plato's cave.
SP: Yeah. And you almost have the blues and the gospel happening in your life. The good news and the bad news every day, and you continue to survive. What happened, when I came to the City, I didn't have to go to a factory job. I was literate enough to go to the Post Office.

FWJ: You and Richard Wright.
SP: What happened is that when I continued to go to college, they told me I was crazy. They said, "What's wrong with you, boy? [laughter] You got that good job, so why are you going to college?" And I told them that I was not interested in the job. So what's happening with me, I'm trying to use autobiography and biography of family to apply the vernacular and use blues and jazz and improvisational rhythms as a method of telling a story. You know, what would have happened to me in the sixties was that I thought I was writing black, but by the year 2010 or so I realized that what I was looking at was a kind of improvised music linguistic model that had come from how African Americans had lived in various communities, because I had access to both Richard Wright and Muddy Waters.

FWJ: In the interview with Gibbons you say that Louis Armstrong has two axes, his horn and his voice, and that his voice is even stronger than his horn. Do you, as a poet, have more than one axe? And can you explain what voice means to you as a poet?
SP: I think you can take my last book *Home/Bass* as an example. It is dedicated to Willie Kent, who was born in 1936, and who is the persona of the poems. I bet I followed 90 percent of Kent's shows over eighteen years that he played in Chicago, and maybe I formally interviewed him three or four times. And one of the things that happens when you are a poet . . . I never tried to re-create who I thought the musician was. I tried through a poem to allude to the truth of his music. So my task was always linguistically daunting. How do I place the words that evoke that? And two things happened.

First, they make you conscious of the fact that you are a professor. Just being an African American does not mean that you have a totality of their experience. You know, you're tenured. You understand the game, but it's capricious. You know, why is it that you don't understand it? And second, I realized that as a poet I did not know that the truth of that experience could be told. I really did not know how much insight I had into that music I got because I studied it or how much I got because he said it to me. I couldn't surmise that I thought he said that. I don't know that I thought that, because this was over eighteen years that he was in a whole lot of incidents. He said things, and I said that in that case the persona has to be a blues singer. He cannot be a poet.

And that makes me think of some of the historical stuff. If I go to Mississippi, I'm absolutely appalled that in Natchez in Adams County in 1827 or '28 there were more millionaires per square mile than anywhere else, including New York City. But there is no evidence that black people were ever there.

FWJ: Can you describe the instruments that you have used in your poetry since you published your first book in 1971?
SP: One thing I have to say. In reading the Beat poets—I know the Beats primarily through the first two volumes of LeRoi Jones's work—there's something about ellipsis and the line, how you think a poem would go on in one direction and then it abruptly changes direction. I learned a great deal and experimented a great deal with that.

FWJ: You point to writers who are quite diverse, such as Gwendolyn Brooks, T. S. Eliot, James Baldwin, Ralph Ellison, and Langston Hughes as being influences on your work. Among these quite different writers, is there a common thread that influenced you most?
SP: Maybe how they invent and use language. I mean, I didn't approach T. S. Eliot as a scholar, but there were things that were said in the early part of "The Waste Land." His imagination is almost . . . like some poets can write about the Milky Way, and it looked like he had the command to write about the galaxy. [laughter] I mean his understanding of what you could do with language. I was intrigued there. And the same thing with Brooks. It's different, because I had studied Romantic poetry and knew something about the sonnet and the ode, and I found that using that high diction to describe people in the kitchen, it looked like the language was out of place. The way she ascribed that language to people in the kitchen I thought was absolutely

miraculous. And another thing, I thought that she had a love affair with black people and accepted them. So the different influence in her was her use of language and eloquence. But Eliot has what I thought Leontyne Price had. I thought Eliot had that kind of precision with language. See, you hear language. I have to hear language. I don't analyze it. When I was hearing how the language was written, maybe Elliot and Derek Walcott. I read Walcott later in my life, and he had an absolute command of the language, absolute command of the language. And that was not what I wanted to be, but I understood that I had to aspire to make my language do whatever that was.

FWJ: Good. Can we return now to that other question? You started elaborating on it. For the reader who is just being introduced to your poetry, what advice would you give as to the way you would like your work read and understood, and what clues do you give to the reader in the poetry as a guide to help read it well and understand it?
SP: I think that the first thing is that for me the English language is a work in progress. Vocabularies, dictionaries—all that stuff is subject to change. The way I phrase and the way I play, and sometimes the breaks in my poetry will feel there is a meaning. I mean there's always a meaning to play. You may not choose to play, you know. I'm in fact playing with the language. I mean musician do that. I try to hear the language differently. I'm hearing it in a certain way. I'm not hearing it entirely. I'm someone who has been exposed to the West and absolutely educated in the African American vernacular. I cannot be Paul Laurence Dunbar. I'm not a book poet, but work with what I think are the most advanced possibilities of black vernacular in terms of what has been done in music, in particular that form of music that is jazz played or sung by a master like Sarah Vaughn or Louis Armstrong. That's what I'm always trying to do.

To me, just telling the story is only part of the point. It is the means to telling the story that's as important as the story I'm telling.

FWJ: Should the reader who's reading your poems read them aloud? Is that important?
SP: I'm a poet of the ear. You know, I don't know how other poets operate, but for some reason I hear the language before I conceive it. That's the language. You know, it goes back to years ago when I first read *The Iliad* and *The Odyssey*. And then somebody brought me *The Divine Comedy*. And even that was sixty some years ago, and the professor was saying that one of the reasons the language of Homer was such that I thought in Greek it

would have been dactylic hexameter. [laughter] And Milton used some of
the same line. So I'm encouraged by the fact that what you do in the line
defines what the poet is about. And I really am blown away by the Greeks.
They are very intelligent, but the way they would use all of these metaphors
and these long lines. . . . It seems to me by the time I get to the African
American experience in music, everything is abbreviated. And so the question is, "How can I have an effect with that mandate that it be abbreviated?"
That's the cause of the problem, because you're hearing it. I'm hearing it, but
I'm hearing it through a specific background of watching all these musicians
and taking notes. In the last fifty years, the great jazz and blues musicians
. . . I have watched them night after night and took notes. In fact, I never had
any intention of doing a book on Von Freeman or Fred Anderson. And then
I looked up and I had all these notes I'd written down over twenty years.
And when I wrote the notes down . . . I mean, it's interesting. When I wrote
the notes down and I had the slashes, I told the editor that if the virgules or
slashes were a problem then remove them. I said I would not use the virgule
if they could make a comma bigger. [laughter]

FWJ: Sterling, you emphasize in that memoir/interview you did with Reginald Gibbons that a work ethic is extremely important to a writer. What
exactly do you mean by a work ethic? Is this like a person who gets up at
6:00 a.m., has a long commute, arrives at the office at 8:00, then at 5:00 goes
home and forgets about it?
SP: You know, for me, that's part of it. But the creative endeavor is deceptive when it pertains to a literary project. You cannot be ever satisfied with
what you have done. When you wake in the morning the routes to where
you need to go do not exist. And that's what a work ethic is, you see. You
cannot write for what might be one year, five years, or ten. You see, you can't
just wake up and say I'm going to write *The Old Man and the Sea*, [laughter]
and you hope you can find yourself in that part of the ocean where you do it.
You have to believe that you can work your way out of this chaos with some
use of craft. I think that understanding craft is what allows you to finish a
project. Let me give you an analogy. One of the things that everybody talks
about is the gift of African American athletes. You see what Michael Jordan
did. I can tell you this from experience. The moves that Michael Jordan had,
he'd better have had them, otherwise these black boys would slap that stuff
back at him. [laughter] It's not easy. And that's the problem with art because
you are dealing with long tradition, and the possibilities of seeing what you
can and cannot do does not reside with you. Other poets have gone for a

long number of years without writing. And you have to keep that in mind. You know, there were times when I could not write for six months. But I tried. What you learn is this: well, that was six months that I was out of it, but sooner or later I began to hear words and examine what I had done and said maybe this is the way.

Whatever people say about me, I will always use craft as the basis of generating texts. That's part of the work ethic. I have never been a preacher. I love the Black Arts Movement. But I don't know how important black was. You know, the two things that stand out in the black experience for me are that there is nowhere in any black community that if you have a band playing and a white musician comes up, they would say don't let him play because he's white. What the band's going to say is, "Can he play?" The other thing is that there's no player on any playground, I don't care how high the racism, that tells a white he cannot play. The question is, "Can he throw a ball?" This leads me to believe that there's something beyond whatever color you are that you have to master.

The other thing is, I could read Latin as well as I could read English. The only thing is that when you read, you understand how these phrases come together because you can't just say one word. I never tried to measure myself as a poet. It's very funny. I don't know who has won a Nobel Prize; I only know what I have read. The two best writers I read of the Americas . . . I don't think that anybody is close to Faulkner in the novel . . . and although I can't read his poetry in the original, I give Neruda an edge over Eliot because that man could absolutely sing. So what you identify with is what you aspire to be.

FWJ: Thank you, Sterling, for that generous response. Here's a final question. It's obvious that history is central to your poetry and that psychology also plays a role. You studied both in college. You did not study creative writing formally, but the fact that you have successfully practiced it and taught it throughout your long career might be an anomaly for younger writers who are majoring or minoring in creative writing in college. Can you describe this alternative path you took to writing?

SP: The creative writing really began when I was maybe in high school, and I wrote a poem. I believe it was a sonnet. I can remember the nun telling me, "But Sterling, poets are born." I replied to the sister, "I was born, too." [laughter] It's deceptive, the way I learned to write, in odd ways. When I was a freshman in college, the only African American writer I came in contact with was James Baldwin in his short story "Sonny's Blues." And it was the first time that I knew you could use that language and that experience to make literature. And shortly thereafter I became a full-time worker at the Chicago Post Office, which allowed me to buy all the books of James Baldwin; someone told me that he had been mentored by Richard Wright. And so I read all the books by Richard Wright. And then somebody told me that the person who had opened doors for Richard Wright and all African American writers was Langston Hughes. And so I began to systematically read texts and philosophies, because I understood that Hughes used historical materialism. That's how you had to understand his world.

FWJ: Sterling, you emphasize the importance of a writer's making connections in life experiences and in reading. In fact, you have continued to extend and enrich your connections by travel into different cultures, such as South Africa in the nineties prior to the presidency of Nelson Mandela when you met Dennis Brutus and other anti-Apartheid writers. Clearly, the journey for you is never over. Thank you, Sterling, for sharing these insights into your life and work with the readers of *FWJ*.

Home/Bass: An Interview with Sterling D. Plumpp

John Zheng / 2014

From *Poetry South* (2014): 22–34. Reprinted by permission of *Poetry South*.

Sterling Dominic Plumpp, born on January 30, 1940, in Clinton, Mississippi, is a blues poet and essayist living in Chicago. He has authored thirteen books including *Half Black Half Blacker; Black Rituals; Blues: The Story Always Untold; Blues Narratives; Clinton; Horn Man; Ornate with Smoke; Velvet BeBop Kente Cloth;* and most recently *Home/Bass.* Plumpp's poetry was included in *The Best American Poetry 1996.* He was Chicago's poet laureate and received the Carl Sandburg Literary Prize for Poetry. He is also the editor of two anthologies, *Somehow We Survive* and *Steel Pudding.* Plumpp is professor emeritus at the University of Illinois at Chicago where he taught in the African American Studies and the English Department. In 2009, *Valley Voices: A Literary Review* ran a special issue on Plumpp's poetics, his artistic and intellectual development, and his distinctive bluesjazz voice. In 2013, the NEH Summer Institute devoted a two-day session to the discussion and exploration of Plumpp's poetry and aesthetics at Mississippi Valley State University. During his stay at MVSU, we had long chats and decided to have an interview mainly on his poetry collection, *Home/Bass,* published by Third World Press in 2013. This interview was conducted right before *Home/Bass* won the 2014 American Book Award.

John Zheng: Professor Plumpp, can you tell us a bit more about yourself before we begin our interview on your latest poetry book *Home/Bass*?
Sterling Plumpp: Let me begin by noting, I was first published in 1968. The event stemmed from a poem I wrote after marching to Cicero, Illinois, in 1966. A black youth had been beaten to death in Cicero, and Bob Lucas, head of the Chicago chapter of CORE, led a march to protest it. This was the period when Black Power became prominent and shortly thereafter the

Black Arts Movement emerged. Here in this cultural and historical malaise, I began my writing and publishing career. The black experience has always been my work.

Therefore my vision as a writer has undergone metamorphoses: black life, black experience, black aesthetic, and finally to the rural Southern experience of the black peasant. I seemed to have found my voice in moist Mississippi mud as a grandson of a tenant farmer. Though I became a member of the OBAC Writers Workshop and was published in *Negro Digest/Black World* and by Third World Press, my soul, nevertheless, longed for the comfort of the rural black southern experience. That's where blues enters my imagination because nothing I ever came into contact with mirrored the experiences on the mourners' bench that touched and molded me in my efforts to write creatively.

Amiri Baraka and Larry Neal are the two Black Arts Movement poets I admired and cherished. They seem to have forged personal voices out of their experience and they were both experts and inclusive with respect to black culture, especially black music. *Preface to a Twenty Volume Suicide Note* and *Dead Lecturer*, though not technically Black Arts Movement texts, were to me unofficial black aesthetic canons. Baraka's *Black Magic: Collected Poetry* is wonderful. Neal's *Hoodoo Hollerin' Bebop Ghosts* is a magnificent display of cultural craft and vision. In many ways my poetry as a southern inhabitant of this planet is a voice searching tracks of Jones/Baraka and Neal. Nikki Giovanni's *Truth Is on Its Way* recording is also brilliant in its display of music, power, and unique voice.

The two writers I had the most conversational exchanges with prior to the appearance of *Home/Bass*'s creation were Leon Forrest and Keorapetse Kgositsile. Forrest—whose *Divine Days* is arguably the finest novel by a Chicago writer—cautioned me not to be afraid to get in the ring with champions. He warned what Ellison had observed that perhaps the reason some writers insisted on being "black writers" was perhaps because they feared the textual champions of world literature. He cautioned me, always, not to be afraid to explore the angularity of the black experience. Observing that "the bookshelf is not an equal opportunity player."

Kgositsile, poet laureate of South Africa, read many of the poems in *Places and Bloodstains* to me in his native Setswana and sometimes in Zulu. There is an aspect of language you can only hear. You need only ears to know, judge, and select it as primary. There is something in Willie Kent I hear that propels me to craft a persona in my poems. It is a personal hearing I seek.

Blues is that authentic something culturally one discerns in the great blues performers and a lot of it has to do with cadence, speech delivered in a personal, unique way. That is what I am grabbing at with slashes or line breaks and construction of a blues singer's persona or a horn's for that matter. It is something so real, so tangible, yet so elusive.

JZ: Thank you for sharing your black life and experience which has been important to your writing. Third World Press published your poetry book, *Home/Bass*, in 2013. Can you give a little history about writing this book?

SP: *Home/Bass* grew out of my preoccupation with blues and with blues singers. I was always fascinated by the power and authority blues singers and ministers had with relationship to the word. I was also wedded to the poignancy of the speech of the rural vernacular of tenant farmers. I had been twenty-nine years in various blues clubs in Chicago when I met Willie Kent in 1988. There was something unrehearsed in his dialogue and manner. I was also in the shadows, so to speak, of *Blues: The Story Always Untold* published in 1989. Willie's voice and performance demeanor placed him squarely in deep blues. I immediately became attracted to him and his music and followed him from 1989 until his death in 2006.

Kent performed from an expansive songbook and almost never repeated a song on a nightly engagement. His utterance fell on ears with the potency of prayer or a sermon. It wasn't long before I recognized the journey we both had taken from cotton fields in Mississippi to Chicago. Kent's music and performance—as it were—became an aesthetic wardrobe that forced me to hear the possibility of poetry in a slightly different light. Listening to him was almost like eaves dropping on a secret conversation he was having with destiny or God. I began taking notes on what his music evoked as memory and experience. In this manner I stumbled upon lines that I tried to nuance with "line breaks." This was *Home/Bass*'s beginnings.

JZ: *Home/Bass* is dedicated to Willie Kent, the blues musician playing bass. Can you talk about your friendship with him?

SP: I was undoubtedly Kent's most loyal fan and admirer. I followed him during his Wednesday and Thursday night gigs at Blues Chicago: 636 and 736 N. Clark respectively. I would talk with him before shows. I also was present at his Friday and Saturday night gigs at both Blues Chicago clubs. I was at his Monday night and weekend gigs at B.L.U.E.S. and his weekend gigs at Rosa's, Legends, Brady's, the Checkerboard, and Boss Man's. I was always dabbling and wrote three songs which Willie recorded: "911" (Delmar), "Address in the Street" (Delmar), and "Lonely, Lonely Streets" (Blue Chicago). I handed Willie's songs and sometimes later he'd say, "I got something for you" and it would be a song recorded on CD.

The French film, *We Are the Blues*, recorded me reading a draft of *Home/ Bass* and Kent and Eddie C. Campbell, playing in the background. In the final months of Kent's life, I along with a female blues singer friend of Kent contributed financially to his support. Kent once said he didn't know I was writing about him. I told him he needed to know he was singing the best blues in Chicago or in the world for that matter.

JZ: Where did you first meet Willie Kent in Chicago in 1988?

SP: I first met Kent while he was playing a gig at Brady's on the Southside of Chicago. I think he had one LP, "I Am What You Need." His power and brilliance was memorable.

JZ: In what way has Kent's voice helped you "invent a blues singer persona narrating" *Home/Bass*?

SP: More than anything else Kent's musical forte anchored my imagination around concepts such as tone, rhythm, a wry, subtle insinuation and irony, ritual, and heritage. Kent re-enacted African American memory and heritage. He reaches deep into the tool kit of the black church's myriad expressions to celebrate and atone. I can honestly say his exhibiting blues through his performances left me no choice but to attempt to construct a persona where the blues performer's voice was on par with the poet's or prophet's. It was only when I struggled to erect a persona for Kent that I felt I was realizing something indelible in my culture.

JZ: So, can we say the voice of *Home/Bass* is a combination of yours and Kent's?

SP: Yes, we can at once say that the voice of *Home/Bass* is a combination of mine and Kent's and the blues greats: Robert Johnson, John Lee Hooker, Howlin' Wolf, Muddy Waters, Elmo James, and Junior Wells whose recordings are canons of American music.

JZ: In the poem "From the Delta," you present Willie Kent in a voice of the first person character:

Max
Well/Street.
Where/I
Got/my name:
HOME/BASS,

West/Side Story.
Got
part/of me
in it. I/come
here/from Delta.

Boston
Blackie/I know.
Children
killing/children.
I/know.
Children
Killed/by children.
I/know.
Children
in trouble/my children.
And/I
know. (*Home/Bass* 11)

Do you try to revive his voice by using the blues skills such as refrain?
SP: Yes, I do. But do this by not creating within a traditional blues form. I try to avoid cliché by not permitting too much repetition or rhyme.

JZ: What was Kent's voice like as a blues singer?
SP: Kent easily possessed the poignancy of an Elmo James. He was not so much a minister delivering a sermon but a member of the flock who done been possessed by the truth that he must give his testimony about. Kent, like Big Daddy Kinsey, evinces a blues experience, even before he utters a sound, possessing a sharecropper's shoulders and hands of a laborer, he convinces you he has the right to talk about the trials and tribulations he done undergone.

JZ: And how did his voice and bass form a unique music that touched you?
SP: Since Kent is a bassist, he controls tempo and texture of his music. He possesses a concept of music and his playing imposes that on songs as well as the ensemble he engages with. There is a rhythmic articulation between bass and drum that creates a unique melodies space for Kent to swing.

JZ: Willie Kent's song, "Born in the Delta," tells his birthplace: "I was born in the Delta, a hundred miles south of the Tennessee line; I was chopping and picking cotton 'way before the age of nine." Kent was born in Inverness, Mississippi. Were many Chicago blues musicians Mississippi Delta émigré?
SP: Many Chicago blues musicians were from the Delta or "the country" as Buddy Guy might say. They were born and grew up in rural communities where their families were engaged in agricultural endeavors centered around cotton. Muddy Waters, John Lee Hooker, Elmo James, John Primer, Otis Rush, Rice Miller, Howlin' Wolf, Carey Bell, and Buddy Guy are names of those whose birthplace is rural agricultural communities of the South.

JZ: When the Delta-style blues went to Chicago, it must have had to adjust itself to the city life. In what way can Willie Kent's voice be both of the Delta and Chicago's West Side?
SP: Since Kent's passion and sincerely felt delivery of lyrics that he makes personal possession is a force of his ability, it positions him to utter lyrics a cappella or unadorned country style. It also allows his brilliant melody delivery to co-exist well with the rhythmic dialogue of bass and drum and guitar.

JZ: What's the typical characteristic of the urban blues?
SP: To me, Chicago urban blues is noted for its beat, something understated and intimate between symmetry of the bass and drums.

JZ: *Home/Bass* also encompasses the voices of other musicians; am I right? Who are the other blues musicians you feel to have a strong connection with?
SP: The other musicians are many, though I will single out the voice of Otis Rush and the guitar work of Buddy Guy. Rush's performances sets the bar for their poignancy and Guy's guitar seems always in want of another galaxy to explore after mapping this one's possibility. Willie Dixon's voice seems to close floodgates of pain just prior to drowning audience and Lurie Bell's originality and skill at playing and singing is epic. I find Sons of Blues (SOB)

and Billy Branch in the pocket, blue, and eager to synthesize the new and the old. Junior Wells's brilliance continues to inspire my imagination. Carl Weathersby, in finding his voice, redeems black music diversity and expands possibility for those who know soul and R&B.

JZ: Did they also impact your writing? In what way?

SP: These other brilliant blues artists constantly remind me that excellence in blues is diverse and that the music itself is in capable hands awaiting meticulous scholarship and appreciation. I see the wide and widening landscape of blues and try to convey the geographic journey that it has recorded. That forces me to try to be imaginative and open to new possibilities of expression as I struggle to "put my mouth to paper."

JZ: I feel that your poetry is a spoken-word type that's strong for performance with music. Can you talk about any significant performance of your poetry? How did the audiences respond to your poetry?

SP: When I recently read in Chicago with Matthew Skoller on harmonica in the background, the audience spoke well of the collaboration. Also, when they filmed *We Are the Blues* with Willie Kent on bass and Eddie C. Campbell on guitar, the commentary regarding the poetry was outstanding. This was also the opinion of those who saw the film on European television. Blues music energizes the poems of *Home/Bass* and brings another dimension to them.

JZ: I also feel that the line break or the word break with slashes in your poetry highlights the line or the word for special attention to the new meaning. Can you use a poem to illustrate this intention?

SP: "On Credit" where the slashes connotes a unique cadence rather than a pause and where the length of line connotes a speech style.

All

ways/I paint
my songs
in my eyes
where they pose.
Life
sized and testifying
ice and fire.
I take

my time and
a little of yours.

Photograph/my
cries. From behind
my eyes.
Shoot
them in color
because
black and
white.

Might.

wanna
fight.

I
can take
a table spoon/full of week
ends.
Make
it
last six whole
months.
Be
cause I wrestled a river
from between some devils
teeth.
When I
was five. Swallowed
it
down with muddy
waters.

I
cry
showers every
time I hear my heart
break. (*Home/Bass* 46–47)

JZ: Section One of *Home/Bass* focuses on Maxwell Street which functions as a mecca for people of different races, as presented in "Gathering Place":

> This
> is the palimpsest/of
> traveled roads. Here.
> Dreams/open
> their arms/wide.
> This
> Is where shadows/hold
> national assemblies.
> . . . .
> This
> is the place/where
> you get/your naturalized
> papers/of
> feelings
>
> Hope
> is the/ruling
> party here. In this/city
> state of/make-a-way-some
> how citizens.
>
> Max
> Well/Street gathers
> voices. While A
> merica/is a land
> where/strangers meander. (*Home/Bass* 21–22)

These poetic lines must present your impression of the street. What is the most significant experience of yours in this gathering place?

SP: The most important experience of mine in this "gathering place is witnessing vendors from many nationalities making a way for their families. A Jewish woman once took me down Halsted between Thirteenth and Fourteenth Streets showing Jewish symbols and relating to me how and when Jewish vendors came there. There were also Middle Eastern vendors and many of the vendors and customers were Hispanics with several generations of a family present—child, parent, grandparent. Most important to me was hearing Jimmie Lee Robinson relate how he grew up in the Maxwell Street community and how Jesse Owens had been at his elementary school to inspire black youth. I also have fond memories of talking to Maxwell Street Jimmy and Willie James.

JZ: Did Maxwell Street also function as a base for Kent's bass music and energize his voice?
SP: Yes, the fact that Maxwell Street was a place where blues musicians could perform and showcase their talents made Maxwell Street a special place for *Home/Bass*. I was told that sometimes Jewish merchants would leave coal outside during winter. This is a perfect place for his bass and for Kent to invite his voice to intone affirmation. Yes, Maxwell Street is a base for Kent to use his bass and energize his voice.

JZ: Jimmie Lee Robinson, a Chicago-born blues musician, called the Maxwell Street Market "a holy place." Are there any bluesy memories of the market that stand out in your mind?
SP: I fondly recall the blues singer nicknamed "the Walker" meandering from place to place with an identity given by those who know the place. I enjoyed Willie James with his family as the band. Maxwell Street Jimmy had a name from out of his association with place. The mixture of folks on Maxwell Street was wonderful. I was there from 1980 until the day it was shut down.

JZ: How was your state of mind in writing from Kent's perspective different from writing other poetry books of yours?
SP: I was more cognizant that literary texts were one way to articulation and working with one's hands was another. I became more appreciative of those who craft a vision, a language, a poetic meaning out of their experience in song and performance.

JZ: The last two stanzas of "Rituals" in section 3 of *Home/Bass* give a vivid description of the two blues musicians:

I/saw
lightning/strike Buddy
Guy/and he squeezed/its
neck/till a D-natural:
Lord/have mercy/on me.

Wrung/its head
off. He/put the
rest/on his guitar/for
strings. Played/warm hail
down/on Theresa's floor.
But/Junior Wells/done
cut the/lightning/fore Buddy
stringed it.

Magic
Slim/is funny.
He
collects/vipers.
Uses/fangs
for picks. Fits/the spinal
columns/on his guitar.
As strings. I/saw him
mad/with a rattler/a
round/his little finger. As/a
slide. That's/why he called
The Hiss Doctor. (*Home/Bass* 100)

The descriptions given in Kent's voice take us inside the blues performance. Did Kent often share with you his comments on other blues musicians? And how did you dramatize his voice?

SP: Kent talked about Robert Johnson, Muddy Waters, Elmo James, and Howlin' Wolf. The foremost thing in my mind as I attempt to dramatize Kent's voice is the myriad ways hyperbole is utilized in blues. There is also humor and a sense of someone masterful narrating something simple.

JZ: Other than influences from Chicago blues musicians, who else have been your literary influences?

SP: My major literary influences have been James Baldwin and Richard Wright. Baldwin because of insistence on writing from one's personal experiences, of squeezing not water but wine from it. And Wright because I knew the landscape of his upbringing and had to somehow learn to wring meaning from meaningless suffering I had known. Ellison taught me to view the epic achievements of those inventing and performing blues, jazz, and gospel. In his way, Charlie Parker forced me to always allow for another more unique way of expressing what I aspired to express.

JZ: Thank you for your time, Professor Plumpp. Is there anything else you'd like to add about *Home/Bass* or Willie Kent?

SP: *Home/Bass* is an important excerpt from a larger work, *Mfua's Song*, about matrilineal ancestors, basically in the narratives of females. I am indelibly connected to the moans and dreams of ancestors who do not know how to quit. Kent is a friend and a metaphor for artists who pry open silence and intone songs from delinquent tongues of generations.

Muddy Waters: A Conversation with Sterling D. Plumpp

John Zheng / 2015

From *Arkansas Review* 46.3 (2015). Reprinted by permission of *Arkansas Review*.

This interview was conducted in two parts, with a focus on Muddy Waters, a Mississippi-born, Chicago blues musician who has had a profound influence on Sterling Plumpp's poetry. The first part was conducted on February 28, 2015, after the Natchez Literary and Cinema Celebration Conference. That day Sterling and I were sitting in my car on the site of Grand Village of Natchez Indians, waiting for the two Fulbright Scholars from Russia and China who were visiting the museum. The second part was continued on March 18, 2015, in my office at Mississippi Valley State University where Sterling Plumpp serves as the writer-in-residence. Plumpp's poetry collection, *Home/Bass*, won the American Book Award in 2014. Special thanks to Seprela Ellis of Mississippi Valley State University for her assistance in making this interview transcription possible.

February 28, 2015

Zheng: Sterling, since the two Fulbright Scholars are visiting the museum, can I do a short interview with you on Muddy Waters while we're waiting for them?
Plumpp: That's fine.

Zheng: Why is Muddy Waters important to your writing?
Plumpp: Muddy Waters exemplifies the evolutionary sect of the blues from the countryside style of the Mississippi Delta originated by Charlie Patton and Robert Johnson to the electric style that he made famous in Chicago. He is undoubtedly the architect of the blues genre and his songs are more

142

or less the iconic text of blues. Another thing about Muddy Waters is that early in his career he found a dedicated African American audience from the thousands who had left Mississippi, found menial, manual labor jobs in the North, and made a new life. They found a kind of healing in his music and because they were so faithful to him in buying his records and supporting his performances, he eventually caught attention of a wide national and international audience. I was at his funeral, and he was so popular to us literally I stood in line several hours to view his body, with many African Americans there on King Drive and 44th Street in 1983.

Zheng: Were you personally his friend?
Plumpp: I was not personally his friend. I never spoke to him. When I initially heard blues, he was the man; he was the artist who moved me the most. I must have seen him fifty to seventy different times in different venues on the west side of Chicago, south side of Chicago, upscale clubs such as Mr. Kelly's, and blues festivals. I was a student of blues and he was one of my favorite subjects.

Zheng: How about his performances?
Plumpp: Very moving, very inspirational, and I always came away awed by his magnificent ability to both play and sing.

Zheng: So in some way, he has blues-ed your mind?
Plumpp: That is correct. To put it in another way, he was the blues priest who baptized me culturally into blues.

Zheng: Can you explain how your poems reflect his blues music?
Plumpp: I think that I'm essentially a cadence or rhythmic line poet and also a metaphoric poet, and how a metaphor is used in blues is that often a very simple metaphor gets in the blues musician's imagination and through the use of hyperbole, they become very meaningful. I think that that is in my mind as I write poetry. The other aspect of it is the whole concept of line. I tried to evoke blues without actually using the blues verse. You know the blues verse is, "I got up this morning and got me a jug and I laid back down. Woke up this morning, got me a jug, and I laid back down." Plus the line, "I was looking for the future and the blues was all I found." I tried to evoke that without actually adhering religiously to that pattern, and I suspected Muddy Waters is the first blues artist that got me to think about how I could actually use blues as part of the craft I'm trying to effect the poem.

Zheng: How about your visit to his hometown and the blues markers in the Delta?

Plumpp: What strikes me is not only Rolling Fork but also the various markers that proclaim the births of blues singers. What catches my eye is the land and the interconnected plantation community which in effect interconnected African American communities in this whole civil war time where that area called the Delta, where that agricultural workers were primarily African Americans, and where the population was primarily African Americans so that you literally had a notion, so to speak, of these African Americans working on plantations and they could move from plantation to plantation. Therefore, if one is an artist he didn't have to go far to find a willing artist. I suppose I was most struck by Dockery Plantation. Not so much about what I saw, but what was said. Here you had a plantation that had a post office. It's an entire entity and apparently the priority of the plantation allowed those who worked there the kind of space where they could actually perform because Charlie Patton would go there, and Robert Johnson would go there. There was something about the way that place was constructed. Muddy Waters is a great blues artist, but I try to separate out of my mind what actually happened in the place of his birth from what happened in the recording studio where he was privileged to be one of the first to record and therefore be projected as a blues singer, and he developed into a great man. The entire blues area seems to be plantation owners owning the land, African American agricultural workers and sharecroppers working the land, and they are the people you see in dispersed churches and the remnants of the churches that remind you that there were churches. You see the graves and you see the miles all the way from Clarksdale and the miles all the way down to Vicksburg. I actually think that there is an untold story of how these African Americans forged a culture, much of it sustained by the black church and how those who came from that culture created their music and originally had an audience of people who actually were sharecroppers and who could move from small town to town. Therefore, when they went to original cities such as Memphis and New Orleans, they got recorded, and you had these large African American communities in Chicago and Detroit where this music became the base of what became popular music that some people called rock 'n' roll and somewhat later "rock."

Zheng: Thank you, Sterling, and we're looking forward to your writing of the untold stories in the Mississippi Delta, and the miles after miles of the blues songs or blues music through your blues poetry.

March 18, 2015

Zheng: Sterling, we'll continue our interview. Muddy Waters, who was a native of Rolling Fork, is considered the father of Chicago blues. Can you describe his blues voice?

Plumpp: Muddy Waters is the father of Chicago blues or of urban blues because he brought the electric sound to the country blues. He has a clear voice in African American vernacular that has authority with the word that one would find in a black minister, or a black deacon, or someone from the black church.

Zheng: So in a way, his voice has the characteristic of gospel?

Plumpp: Well, it could be gospel. I say the rural African American church. Gospel would be another way of saying he sounds very much the way black ministers sound in the rural, what they would call, country church.

Zheng: Can you talk about the characteristics of Chicago blues?

Plumpp: Chicago blues is noted for the dialogue or interaction between the base and the drum. There's a definite beat. There's a definite pace. There's a definite beat that's maintained, and that beat allows the melody to reflect in a brilliant way. If that beat is un-tempoed, then it allows that particular music of blues to move closer to what some would call rock 'n' roll.

Zheng: Rock 'n' roll?

Plumpp: It's danceable. What I'm trying to say is, it's a danceable beat. It's a beat that you pop your fingers to. It's a beat that wants to make you move.

Zheng: So, Chicago blues is a combination of blues and rock 'n' roll?

Plumpp: To put it more accurately, Chicago blues is an exploration of the country blues that pushes it to a mode that is consistent with rock 'n' roll. I mean the playing of John Lee Hooker, the playing of Muddy Waters, and the playing of Ike Turner is what the great British musicians play, whether it be the Rolling Stones or Cream. You know, they take that beat. You know, blues I mean. I think that African American blues refers to the attitude of the mood of the song, but musically it's un-tempoed. It's un-tempoed like gospel. You say jazz to the extent that you get brilliant instrumental accomplishment along with it, some obviously in terms of structure, in terms of dynamics. The harmonica player, Lil Walter Jacobs, sounds more like jazz, more like bebop. Muddy Waters, although you cannot readily say that it is jazz, but his sophistication, his use of slide guitar, and his use of other instruments do have an accumulative effect similar to jazz.

Zheng: I remember last time on our way to Clarksdale we talked about the difference between Muddy Waters's blues songs and B.B. King's. Could you say something more about it?

Plumpp: Yes. B.B. King is a brilliant blues man, but B.B. King, to me, performs with a blues orchestra. There are far more pieces, and he augments that great orchestral play both with his voice and with his guitar. B.B. King is fully capable of engaging in what Robert Johnson calls "deep blues," but that doesn't seem to be his forte. His music is somewhat more jovial, at least to me. Muddy Waters, on the other hand, comes from that aspect of blues where the blues singer is almost in a ritual, summoning something from the depth of his soul to relieve the pain or the conflict that he is confronted with.

Zheng: I want to come back to talk about your poetry. How did Muddy Waters influence your poetry?

Plumpp: He influenced me primarily because of how he engaged vernacular. A writer has choices to make in terms of the voice of the persona. Although I was very familiar with Ralph Ellison and his construction of Trueblood, which is the greatest vernacular achievement in literature, I'm not writing fiction. I'm writing poetry, and there is something about both the tone and the phrasing of Muddy Waters that forces me to try and create a line that suggests blues, or to create a line that suggests blues even while a persona is engaged in ordinary dialogue.

Zheng: So, your poetic voice is a creative representation of Muddy Waters?

Plumpp: Muddy Waters is the blues, but Muddy Waters is the marvel, let's put it that way. Muddy Waters influenced me more than anyone else because of his ability to sing the blues.

Zheng: He influenced you more than other blues musicians?

Plumpp: Yes, because of his ability to sing the blues. He sang country blues brilliantly; you know, just him and the guitar. He sang urban un-tempo blues brilliantly. He sang a variety of blues songs extremely well, and he had a brilliant band, sometimes with piano, harmonica, and guitar. It's almost as if when he created his first recording blues band, he set the format that others would follow.

Zheng: Any performance that you had a very good memory of?

Plumpp: My finest memory of Muddy Waters is when he played at a place called Curly's on Madison Street. It was dark, and he played as if he were at Carnegie Hall. He played with his heart, and the people reacted to him as if they were at a revival about to be saved, or as if they were at a church listening to someone preach. I mean there was a tremendous response. They spoke back to him as he was singing. He gave memorable performances. This happened to be an African American community, and the reason why I specify it is because I can have the analogy of the black minister preaching in a country black church and the congregation responding to him and have the black audience responding to Muddy Waters. It's not racial; it's cultural.

Zheng: I know in Chicago, the very famous street is Maxwell Street for blues performances.

Plumpp: Yes.

Zheng: Did Muddy Waters ever play there?

Plumpp: I never saw him there. First of all, it's a flea market. A lot of prominent musicians such as Lil Walter would play there. They would be singing, and they would get gigs. Playing there is an advertisement, and people seeing them play there would say, "I want you to come play for me." Blah, blah, blah. It was a wonderful venue for them to play.

Zheng: On our way to the Emmett Till Museum in Glendora, I said that your poetry had avoided the refrain of blues because refrain may make a poem sound boring. In other words, you keep the blues rhythm, but you avoid its repetition. Is that right?

Plumpp: That is correct. What I try to effect in my poetry is blues moments through the use of rhythm, metaphor, and line break. My use of slashes is that I'm trying to create the kind of pause that you would hear in a blues singer as he's singing. It's an abrupt pause.

Zheng: So, the uses of metaphor and line breaks are the two major characteristics of your poetry?

Plumpp: And maybe the tone.

Zheng: The tone keeps the rhythm?

Plumpp: That's correct.

Zheng: And the metaphor keeps your poetry interesting?
Plumpp: Yes.

Zheng: The line break distinguishes your poetry from other kinds of blues poetry?
Plumpp: Yes. I'm directly influenced by blues performers and not record performance. You know, I spent fifty years of my life witnessing blues singers, and that's what I'm trying to capture. I'm not trying to capture what I heard someone sing on a record.

Zheng: So you go to the place to see the blues musicians perform on the stage.
Plumpp: Yes, and that's what blues is to me. It's this relationship between their audiences, but it's a fifty-year relationship.

Zheng: There's an immediacy between your poetry and the blues music.
Plumpp: Yes. I mean, in fact, it's notes. It's notes in the last book, *Home/ Bass*. There was a discussion with the editor that actually came to stanzas. See, any poet takes notes. And these notes are suggestions. Now when it comes to manuscript, they could become a book. There are some definite questions that have to be asked, and you might have to rewrite. You might have to delete and eliminate. But a great deal of the last book, the way it appears came out of dialogue between me and the editor, Gwendolyn Mitchell.

Zheng: How long has she been the editor at Third World Press?
Plumpp: She's been the editor for, I would say, ten to fifteen years.

Zheng: The refrain in blues is to stimulate a great emotional involvement through the repetition of words. How did you stimulate an emotional involvement or achieve such effect in your blues poetry?
Plumpp: Well, sometimes you do it with hyperbole. Hyperbole is one of the things that makes the blues. In fact, I mean when a blues singer says, "I will have a hard time missing you baby, with my pistol in your mouth. I will have a hard time missing you baby, with my pistol in your mouth. You might be going north, but your brains are staying south." It does not mean that he's going to shoot her. It means that he's telling her that he wants her so badly it is almost as if he would blow her brains out. A lot of that in the blues. I mean the blues is filled with hyperbole.

Zheng: Is there a specific example that you remember from your poetry about using hyperbole?

Plumpp: Well, it's in *Home/Bass*, the portions where the narrator Willie Kent is talking about Magic Slim. At some point I think that he says that Magic Slim uses the fangs of a snake as a slide on his guitar. In other words, he risked being poisoned himself (laughter) in order to play the music. But it's filled with that. I'm just thinking about maybe in the poem, you can come here and in a second you can be killed. It's not intended that it's a dangerous place, but emotionally that's what I said.

Zheng: You have been at Valley for over two months now?

Plumpp: Yes.

Zheng: And you have done several Delta tours. I think three. What impressed you most from your Delta tours of the blues sites? For instance, your visit to the Muddy Waters marker in Rolling Fork.

Plumpp: The most startling thing about visiting the blues sites is the enormity of the plantations. When juxtaposed side by side from Clarksdale to Rolling Fork, my suspicion is that you have very few land owners. That's one. Another thing that impresses me particularly about Rolling Fork is that although Muddy Waters says that is his home, he was not born there. In fact, he was born somewhere in a black community in the rural area. (laughter)

Zheng: And his cabin (a replica) is inside the Delta Blues Museum in Clarksdale.

Plumpp: There are two things. Number one is how anonymous these great blues singers were when they left Mississippi. They were absolutely anonymous. They were just another one of the black peasants in the crowd. Number two is how they achieved such vernacular eloquence in the place where they were. Apparently. How did they achieve that eloquence? How did they find the space given all the forces designed to dehumanize them? How did they find the space to be that eloquent? It's amazing.

Zheng: Toru Kiuchi, the Fulbright Scholar from Japan who went with us to Dockery Farms, said that he always wanted to see Dockery Farms since high school. He said when he was in high school he read something about Dockery Farms, and since then he always had that desire to go. Finally, he went this time, and he was so excited. What would you say about Dockery Farms, which is regarded as the birthplace of blues?

Plumpp: See, my immediate reaction of seeing the space and realizing Robert Johnson, Charlie Patton, Howlin' Wolf, Muddy Waters, I mean the great park staples. . . . Two things come to mind. The gathering of these African Americans on this particular cotton plantation and how much talent was there, number one, and apparently Charlie Patton is the genius who first figured out a way to create a song out of that experience and other people pattern their songs on his song. The second thing that impressed me seems that, at least on this plantation, these citizens had the space. There seemed to be a lack of interference in attempt to produce and carry on this culture. Those are the two things that impressed me the most.

Zheng: One of the essential figures of your recent book, *Home/Bass*, is Muddy Waters. Sometimes he's represented by some other blues musicians in your book, for instance, in chapter 27. How did you think of creating a poetic voice of Muddy Waters in someone else's guise?

Plumpp: Well, I have been fifty years into blues clubs, and originally I saw Howlin' Wolf, Muddy Waters, Otis Rush, Lightnin' Hopkins, and somewhat later Junior Wells, but it became very apparent to me when I followed Willie Kent for eighteen years. I followed him for the last eighteen years of his life. I was so moved by his dedication to his music and his sound that in fact, when I was constructing a persona for Willie Kent, I was really constructing a persona for Muddy Waters because Kent had nearly improvised on the voice, the tensions, and the tones that great Muddy Waters had given us. It is an enormous musical legacy.

Zheng: So far, during your stay at Mississippi Valley State University, have you written any poems about Mississippi or about your homecoming?

Plumpp: I wrote one poem about homecoming, but more importantly the land, the miles and miles of plantation. It takes me directly back to the people who reared me. My grandfather was born in 1880 on a cotton plantation. He reared me. His wife, my grandmother, was born in 1890 on a cotton plantation. They lived their entire lives on cotton plantations. A lesser Dockery Farm is where they lived. They went to the country churches. They're buried less than five miles from the plantation where they had worked all of their lives and where their parents and grandparents had been slaves. I write about the place as being the humus out of which African Americans farm the culture, out of which I try to create my art.

Zheng: You are the native son of Mississippi and your poetry certainly has a voice that you got from Mississippi, or from the country churches or from your grandparents. However, you have lived in Chicago for over fifty years. Your voice is also urban. With all this combination of voices, can we say that your poetry is one that possesses the tones and voices of blues, gospel, and jazz?

Plumpp: That is correct. That's the way I view myself. I think that the act of literacy is an act that automatically estranges one from one's folk roots. I think that whatever happened in my case, I had to rediscover the folk roots of my voice particularly in the blues poems. But in the jazz poems, it means that I had become literate and I had this dual responsibility of achieving a literate persona with a linkage or nuances of this folk cultural heritage.

Zheng: And cultural heritage is reflected in your poetry.
Plumpp: Yes.

Zheng: Thank you, Sterling.
Plumpp: You're welcome.

An Interview with Sterling D. Plumpp

Mamie Osborne / 2015

From Valley Voices: A Literary Review 15.2 (Fall 2015): 31–35. Reprinted by permission of *Valley Voices: A Literary Review.*

Mamie Osborne: Will you describe your work as a writer-in-residence at Mississippi Valley State University?

Sterling D. Plumpp: I am a professor of English and a widely published poet over the last half century. My curriculum vitae speaks for itself. I have given public talks and readings to the students, faculty, and community at large.

MO: What academic assets do you think MVSU expects you to bring to enrich campus life?

SP: I have contacts with institutions around the world and with eminent African and African American authors, nationally and internationally, that I could encourage to come to Valley and conduct workshops for students or faculty, and this would expand the offerings and cultural visibility of MVSU. I believe MVSU expects me to bring visibility to cultural offerings and possibilities for students to excel as well as faculty in African American literature. For instance, when I was in South Africa in 1995, Nadine Gordimer gave a party and signed ten or so of her novels for me. I could offer the MVSU library a signed Gordimer book. Another consideration, I recently read at the Museum of Contemporary Art in Chicago with the AACM. I could encourage them to invite members of the AACM to campus for a concert or symposia.

MO: What courses are you teaching this semester?

SP: I taught classes in world literature and major black writers my initial semester here. I'm teaching a course in creative Writing and a course in modern poetry this semester.

MO: How do you motivate students, especially English majors, in creative writing? And what do you hope your students learn from taking your class?
SP: You expose students to models of good writing. You encourage and work with students on the craft of creative writing and in understanding the language and discipline of the genre. I have taught creative writing at a major university at every level: introductory, undergraduate, and graduate.

MO: You are nationally and internationally known as an essayist and a poet. How do you write a poem? Is there an incubation stage? For example, does a poem first come to you as a concept or topic to explore, or a feeling or an impression you have?
SP: How I write a poem. I am always writing a poem even when I am not writing it down. I am exploring and re-exploring feelings and memories of experiences that might spark a poem. I am always condensing my expression and seeking new ways to find meaning. I hear my poems. I am a poet of the ear. I refine internal meaning many times.

MO: How long does it take to write a poem? To go from an idea or concept in your head to a printed text?
SP: Some of the poems related to music and musicians took decades. *Blues: The Story Always Untold, Horn Man, Ornate with Smoke, Blues Narratives, Velvet BeBop Kente Cloth,* and *Home/Bass,* I like to think, are "lyrical notes" I developed into poems over an extended period of time.

MO: When did you write your first poem? And what was your muse/inspiration to write?
SP: My first published poem was "Black Hands" written after I participated in a civil rights march in Cicero, Illinois, in 1966. The poem was published in *Negro Digest* in 1968. Oftentimes, poems will differ from initial drafts of poems and the published poems which is the combination of many drafts over a period of time.

MO: When did you first think of yourself as a poet?
SP: I first thought of myself as a poet when I was twenty and had finished reading the *Divine Comedy.* I knew I had to, somehow and somewhere, apprentice myself in some course of study, so I could produce texts condensed and memorable.

MO: You have been referred to as an "international blues poet" and "the finest blues poet of this century." Your latest book, *Home/Bass*, won the 2014 American Book Award. Home/Bass fuses blues and jazz rhythms with poetic insight about the black experience, but I recently heard you say something like, "People say I'm a blues poet. That's not what I am." If that is accurate, will you explain what you mean by that statement? And how do you categorize your poetry?

SP: When I say I'm not a blues poet, I mean I am not simply a blues poet. I am self-consciously an American poet writing out of a sense of African continuity in the culture and music specifically of African Americans or blues people. Blues music and the aesthetics of blues attracted my ear because my maternal grandfather (1880–1955) and my maternal grandmother (1890–1993) were devout Christians and fell on bended knees each morning they arose and every night before retiring they prayed aloud to their God or heavenly Father. The cadences, intonation, rhythms, and manner of delivery of their oral prayers came back to me when I heard blues recordings at about the age of five.

I was baptized in a southern black Baptist church and sat on a mourner's bench. The conversionary experience I underwent in being saved had dialogues and language patterns that I later heard in blues. The speakers in both cases had this immense belief in the word and displayed an unparalleled authority in language and usage. Yes, I write blues poems and blues poems with a little education which are jazz poems

MO: What or which writers have influenced you?

SP: Greek tragedies and tragedians: Euripides and Aeschylus had more impact on my imagination than any literary text. However, African Americans such as James Baldwin, Richard Wright, Ralph Ellison, and LeRoi Jones (Amiri Baraka) pointed me in the direction to achieve a personal literary voice. They wrote from the black experience creatively, powerfully, and imaginatively.

MO: Since you were "coming-of-age" as a poet during the 1960s, were you involved in the Black Arts Movement?

SP: I owe my development to the Organization of Black American Culture (OBAC) Writer's Workshop because week after week we met three weeks a month, read our poems, discussed and workshopped each other's poems. More importantly, Hoyt Fuller, editor of *Negro Digest*, was a bibliophile and created a salon for the fledging writers gathered in OBAC. Furthermore, he published some of us and concomitantly wrote letters for some of us to get jobs at universities.

The Black Arts Movement is complex. It was a political and historical awakening that saw African Americans creating forums so that they could discuss and discourse about their philosophies of what they intended to write. It occurred at a time when blacks and other oppressed people were breaking the hold of their masters who had controlled them for centuries. As a literary movement, it was a continuum stretching from the Harlem Renaissance to mid-1960s.

MO: Has your poetry changed over the years?
SP: My poetry has changed a great deal over the years. It has moved beyond consciousness to a meditation on the journey my cultural odyssey has negotiated.

MO: How much do the earlier years of your life inspire your creativity?
SP: I see the earlier years of my life as an apprenticeship with the discovery of the hardship of my days and my memory of it. I greatly expanded on its possibility.

MO: Over the past ten to fifteen years tourism in the state of Mississippi has increased significantly, coinciding with blues trail markers and civil rights trail markers strategically placed throughout the state, most of them throughout the Mississippi Delta. Tourists, including contemporary artists—writers, musicians, visual artists, and photographers—leave the Delta artistically inspired. One recording artist recently won a Grammy award for a song she wrote after visiting the grave of blues singer Robert Johnson, the site of the Emmett Till marker in Money, Mississippi, the Tallahatchie Bridge, and Dockery Farms. Has being back in Mississippi, especially in the Delta, inspired you creatively?
SP: Being back in Mississippi has reinforced my knowledge of how African American culture and vernacular has brilliantly influenced blues which signifies the black determination to live, thrive, and survive. I realize how dedicated blacks have always been to providing education for their children. Valley is a living proof.

MO: Are you working on any writing project while teaching at MVSU? And when did you start this project?

SP: Yes, I am writing a long blues-nuanced poem in voices of ancestors. I began it one week after I commenced teaching in January.

MO: How did you develop the idea for this project?
SP: Since 1980 when my mother passed, I have consciously sought literary genres and techniques to map the contours of vision my ancestors have shared over the last two centuries. The current project flows from and builds on that. The current project is an improvisation and a vision of that aesthetic.

MO: What is your target date for its completion? Or can a writer predict a completion date for a creative project?
SP: I believe every four months sections should be ready for publication. To complete a draft can take years or as long as my time and health will allow.

MO: Finally, how does a Mississippi Delta winter compare with a Chicago winter?
SP: There is no comparison between the memorable landscapes and seasons in the Mississippi Delta to the impromptu harshness reinforced by the alienating influence of vertical living that leaves one a virtual stranger in his community.

The Mississippi Arts Hour: An Interview with Sterling Plumpp and Patrick Oliver

Diane Williams / 2015

From *MPB Radio* (aired August 20, 2015). Printed by permission of the interviewer.

Diane Williams: Welcome to the *Mississippi Arts Hour*. I'm Diane Williams, the host for today's show. Each week we talk with people from around the state who are involved creatively with art, music, crafts, literature, festivals, and cultural events. Today I will be talking with Sterling Plumpp and Patrick Oliver. Sterling is a poet, educator, and critic. He has written numerous books and he was an advisor on the television production of the documentary *The Promised Land*. Patrick is a program manager and literary consultant dedicated to promoting writing as a tool. That and more . . . coming up on the *Mississippi Arts Hour*.

Diane Williams: Welcome to the *Mississippi Arts Hour*. I'm Diane Williams, your host for today's show. It's good to be back in the studio and I have two gentlemen with me today, Sterling Plumpp and Patrick Oliver. The gentlemen have been in town. . . . They've been working with the Margaret Walker Alexander National Research Center doing book signings, book talks, and they're in town also for the Mississippi Book Festival, the first statewide book festival, so they're here for a short period of time. Also, Sterling Plumpp is the artist-in-residence at Mississippi Valley State University. So we'll be talking about those things, but these gentlemen are all about literacy. They're all about poetry, literacy, writing, critiquing, understanding, making a difference on the horizon as it relates to having something to say, something that's meaningful. Sterling Plumpp was born here. He's from Clinton, Mississippi. He's a poet, educator, editor, and literary critic.

He's got numerous books out that I'm sure he'll tell us all about. Some of those are *Horn Man; Ornate with Smoke; Half Black Half Blacker; The Mojo Hands Call, I Must Go.* Sterling, it's good to have you here on the show.
Sterling Plumpp: Good to be here.

Diane Williams: Should I call you Professor Plumpp or is it okay that I call you by your first name?
Sterling Plumpp: My first name is adequate.

Diane Williams: Okay, thank you. So what brought you to Mississippi? I know it wasn't just the festival and the book signing.
Sterling Plumpp: No, about a decade ago I established a relationship with John Zheng, editor of *Valley Voices* and chairman of the English department at Mississippi Valley State. That association led to him publishing a special issue of *Valley Voices* on my work.

Diane Williams: And you are a poet, is that correct?
Sterling Plumpp: I am a poet. Subsequently, over the last decade he has featured my work in four or five different issues of the magazine. And last December, he invited me to join the faculty at Mississippi Valley State University as poet-in-residence and professor of English.

Diane Williams: That is great, and I'm glad to have you here in the state at this time. One of the things that we are proud of at the Mississippi Arts Commission and in the state of Mississippi is our statewide poet laureate. And at this time it's Natasha Trethewey. We will soon be rolling out the application process for someone new to become the 2016–2020 poet laureate for our state. And I hope that is something you'll pay close attention to and other poets around the state as well. I know that you're all about not just writing poetry, but poetry that makes a difference that makes us stand up at attention. Why do you write poetry?
Sterling Plumpp: I feel that the greatest gift human beings have is language, and I think that's how they define and ultimately control the world. Specifically because I'm an African American, which literally means that I came to these shores involuntarily, that I came to these shores as property. I feel it's incumbent upon me to say not so much who I am but who my ancestors were and to say it without the biases of those who packed me in the ships and those who confined me to the fields and tutored me with a whip. So part of my task in life is to use language to speak about the humanity of

African Americans to affirm that humanity and to be proud of the legacy of the people who developed Negro spirituals, blues, jazz, and gospel.

Diane Williams: It sounds like you stand on the shoulders of the ancestors and feel the spirit of those that have come before you through the struggle so that you could be here today, and you haven't forgotten that. That's something we want our young people to understand as well; that because of those Africans that came over, we have an opportunity. We have an opportunity, and we have all the hope in the world to move forward in our lives.

Sterling Plumpp: Yes, my poetry and art is not a complaint. I do not feel that slavery handicapped African Americans in any way. I do feel, however, because I'm not an immigrant that I did not come from Western Europe, from England, Spain, Holland, or France seeking a better life, I did not come with the history of the Roman Empire behind me or a Greek civilization. It is a fact that none of these immigrants from Europe truly produced anything culturally that remotely matches the achievements of Negro spirituals, blues, jazz, and gospel in the world.

Diane Williams: If you're just tuning in, you're listening to the *Mississippi Arts Hour*. I'm Diane Williams, the host for today's show and you just heard the voice of Sterling Plumpp. Also in the studio with me today is Patrick Oliver. He is a program manager and literary consultant dedicated to promoting reading and writing as tools for empowerment. He uses a variety of innovative projects to engage children, youth, and adults through writing workshops, author talks, book discussions, professional development, and community forums. Welcome to the studio, Patrick.

Patrick Oliver: Hey, I am glad to be here with you.

Dianne Williams: You know a few years ago someone—I think in Tennessee, you know Facebook is a wonderful thing—said, "Diane, you need to meet this person, Patrick Oliver." And I think I befriended you on Facebook. I tried to catch up with you when we were in New Orleans for the Essence Festival, and I could not catch up with you. The event was so huge, but finally we caught up at the National Association of Black Storytellers Conference in Chicago, Illinois. Tell me a little bit about your work.

Patrick Oliver: I was born and raised in Little Rock, Arkansas. Very humble beginnings. There were seven of us, seven children I should say. And I had a grandfather who loved to read, specifically the newspaper, so that became my fore way into loving, what Sterling was talking about earlier, language and the importance of it. It's that seeing him on the front porch reading every day, you know like there's something about that. Why is he reading every day? That kind of captured my attention. So I started reading with him every day, and that really opened my eyes to what was going on in the world. I got excited about what I was reading, whether it was sports, whether it was news or world issues. So when I thought about it, it was like, hey, every young person should have that opportunity to kind of read books, newspapers, and magazines and find out what is happening around the world. They may not get there, but at least they have the opportunity to read about what's happening in New York City, what's happening in Memphis, Tennessee, what's happening in Jackson, Mississippi, what's happening in Africa, what's happening in Europe. That became glued to me early on, so that became part of my passion for promoting literature.

Diane Williams: So how did you figure out how to stimulate the young people to want to do that?
Patrick Oliver: It was very difficult. (Laughs) Not easy, particularly when you're talking about the technology world. Involving artists! You mentioned early some of the work that I do around the world. Having people like Sterling Plumpp come to a community. Having people like Tony Medina, having visual artists who've won national awards come to your community. And young people hear their conversations that pretty much reflect their environments. Most writers I work with come from very humble beginnings and very tough situations, so when young people hear those stories they're like, "Wow, that's interesting. It sounds like my neighborhood. That sounds like me. If they did that, maybe I can do the same thing." And many writers I work with, not just poets, but also journalists that I work with. Young people see the connection and the importance of writing in any profession. It could be a contract administrator that I would bring to the program so they can see that connection. Any profession you select, there's a lot of writing and reading associated with it.

Dianne Williams: So you do a radio show as well, don't you?
Patrick Oliver: *Literacy Nation.* I've been on hiatus for six months now. I may start it back. I'm in Chicago running around like crazy to put together a literacy project there.

Diane Williams: So *Literary Nation,* the talk show. Where was that?

Patrick Oliver: Based in Little Rock, Arkansas, KDF Public Radio Show. We interviewed major writers every Thursday for an hour.

Diane Williams: You had people on the show like Marian Wright Edelman; Common, who's a poet and rapper; Hill Harper, the actor; Sonia Sanchez, the poet; Susan Taylor, the publisher; and numerous others. That's incredible.
Patrick Oliver: I try to go after the best. I want to make my show the most listened to show in the country, so I went after the best. It's a matter of, "Hey, I'm a writer," so you submit a proposal and make it sound good, and they respond accordingly.

Diane Williams: That is incredible. We're going to take a little bit of a break and listen to some music. The first selection is by Awadagin Pratt. I really like his piano playing, and this is Prelude by Johann Sebastian Bach.

Diane Williams: Welcome back to the *Mississippi Arts Hour*, I'm Diane Williams, the host for today's show and in the studio with me is Sterling Plumpp and Patrick Oliver, and we've been having an interesting conversation that will only build as the time goes on. Sterling, I've read about you so many times. I received a copy of *Valley Voices*, and I have every copy in my office from the last couple of years. It looks like I see your name in there all the time. Your last name is spelled with two p's. I don't know if that was intentional, was it by birth or did it just happen?
Sterling Plumpp: Legend has it, all the way back to the historical fact that my father was born in 1910. His father was lynched in Dumas, Arkansas. By 1922, his brother migrated to South Bend, Indiana, and there were several generations of Plumpps who worked at a Studebaker factory there. My grandfather apparently had difficulty living within the parameters of "his place."

Diane Williams: As an African American?
Sterling Plumpp: As an African American of Mississippi. He was in trouble, and added a "p" to his name.

Diane Williams: Okay.
Sterling Plumpp: By the time I was born it was spelled with two p's. My father's name was spelled with two p's. I was constantly corrected by extremely well educated people that were trying to tell me that the second p

didn't make any sense, and I told them it didn't make any difference but that was my name.

Diane Williams: And that's something for you to be proud of, the reason why your dad did that. Tell me about your upbringing in Mississippi.
Sterling Plumpp: I was born on a cotton plantation outside of Clinton. The address was Clinton, Mississippi, Route 1, Box, Tinnin Road, blah, blah. In 1940, I was born to a mother who had had one son under her maiden name, and I was the second. The tradition, at least in my family, was since she was not married, I was raised completely by my grandparents. In fact, I have absolutely zero recognition of my mother as being my mother. Somewhere around the age of three or four my grandmother had to introduce her to me as being my mother. I thought my mother was my grandmother's daughter. Very religious household. Both grandparents prayed aloud each night before they went to bed, prayed aloud each morning when they arose.

Diane Williams: That's incredible.
Sterling Plumpp: And prayed aloud when there was some kind of threatening contingency such as an approaching storm, or during World War II when the letter from my uncle was late. People don't understand what World War II was; so many people got killed in World War II. If the letter from him was not on time it could mean that he was dead, or if you got a letter from the army, that was the reason for apprehension. "Are they writing to tell me that my son is dead?" It was a hideous war, it was not Desert Storm, and it was not Vietnam. It was an absolutely brutal war and millions of people died. I grew up in that household. It was a household where the mean education of grandparents was maybe second to the fourth grade. Bare literacy. I was not sent to school at all until I was eight years old because the round trip distance to the school would have been five miles, and my grandmother did not want to put a child through that task until they were "big enough to take care of themselves." And you would walk, and so therefore for the remainder of my school year I was two years behind all of the students without flunking. The most poignant thing I learned about being the oldest child in class . . . awkward, large, being country; that is retaining the vernacular of the things that I learned. I realized that if you are smart people will get off your back.

Diane Williams: So you didn't have to fight, if you were smart?
Sterling Plumpp: The few academic people will get off your back.

Diane Williams: So that spurred you on?
Sterling Plumpp: Yeah, they would get off your back. They would not make fun of you if you could best them in subjects. They will hate you, they'll resent you, but the laughter is gone.

Diane Williams: So you excelled in your education and went on to college?
Sterling Plumpp: I graduated at the age of twenty; eventually I went to a liberal arts college in Kansas, Saint Benedicts, where I was introduced to literature. You know, get a hint of it. When I say I was introduced, that is an understatement. We read maybe five different tragedies by people like Euripides, *The Iliad*, the entire *Divine Comedy*, *Paradise Lost*, the Romantic poets, whatever Western literature is, those made the text; we read Chaucer. Some people get literacy confused with learning to read and write. This constructed an entirely different world for me than the world as a Christian black boy. I know I learned that there was an entirely different way of viewing human beings in society simply through reading, and I wanted to contribute whatever I could to that worldview by learning how to write.

Diane Williams: You're listening to the *Mississippi Arts Hour*, MPB Radio, and I'm talking to Sterling Plumpp. This is Diane Williams. Also in the studio with me, a little quiet right now, but that's my fault, is Patrick Oliver. Patrick, tell me a little bit more about the work that you're doing. Bring us up to date.
Patrick Oliver: To date? The work that I'm currently doing?

Diane Williams: Well, bring us up to that point.
Patrick Oliver: I'm working in Chicago right now. I'm working on a project with the Steans Family Foundation. It's kind of happening around the country with K-3rd grade reading. A lot of organizations, school districts, and businesses are looking at what are the literacy issues in our communities and how do we address it. So a lot of foundations and corporations are getting together and saying, "Hey, this is not just a school education issue. This is an issue that a city has to deal with or a state has to deal with because if we're not producing literate individuals, how are we going to compete nationally? How are we going to compete with folks around the world? How do we get contracts to our community if we can't say that we have a literate community?" Organizations and cities and states are recognizing that.

Diane Williams: So you agree with what Sterling said that it's not just reading and writing?

Patrick Oliver: It's not just reading. It's beyond reading and writing. It's about survival. It's about how we get young people to get those basic skills so they can survive in this competitive world today.

Diane Williams: . . . an understanding about life, an understanding about the world around us, from what I'm understanding Sterling to say.

Patrick Oliver: It's very important that young people understand that. You know how Sterling said the importance of language and what language can do for young people, and how it can improve the lives of young people . . .

Diane Williams: So what kind of strategies are you using to do that? Do you have a matrix? Do you have a program, a booklet, or a guide for the young people? What are your strategies?

Patrick Oliver: We have a number of things. I tell people all the time, "Literacy is not a young people issue, that's an adult issue." Because young people are onto the strategies of adults, so we have to get very creative and smart in our strategies as adults. How do we get creative as adults to get young people excited about literature? So again, something I talked about earlier was making sure that we expose young people to writers like Sterling, and expose their parents. Make sure their parents are excited for what we're about to engage their young people in. We have a parent-engagement component that we're going to push really hard and we will have those parents meet the writers that I'm talking about, to be a part of these community discussions that we're going to have with writers to expose young people. We're going to spend a lot of money on books to make sure young people have books. We're going to give them books. We're going to work with the American Library Association and the Hispanic Library Association, and the Blackout Association. All of these various associations, and ask them to support what we do. Make sure every child has a library card. If you can't afford books, the library has free books for you, so we're making sure that happens.

Diane Williams: It sounds like a lot of work, but it sounds like a lot of important work that you'll be doing.

Patrick Oliver: Important and fun, to work with young people. People say, "Patrick, why do you smile all the time?" If you work with a group of kids all of the time you can't do anything but smile because of the things they say, the things they do, what they come up with. We have a great time, so I look forward to the work that I do because of that exposure to young people.

Diane Williams: We're going to listen to a little bit of music right now. This time we're going to listen to Cassandra Wilson from her CD called *Lovely* and the selection is "Lover Come Back to Me."

Diane Williams: Welcome back to the *Mississippi Arts Hour.* I'm Diane Williams, the host for today's show. Generally I work at the Mississippi Arts Commissions Office as the director of grants, so give us a call if you're interested in applying for the upcoming mini-grant round. The deadline is November; the process opens up in October. Also, one of the things that will be rolling out towards the fall of this year is our poet laureate selection. It will be an opportunity for great poets to apply to be our state poet laureate. Currently, Natasha Trethewey is the poet laureate who went on to become both the Mississippi poet laureate and the national poet laureate. That is very unusual, so that gives you an idea of the type of applications we're look-ing forward to receiving. It is our beliefs, and when I say "our," we're working with cultural organizations in the state such as the Mississippi Humanities Council, Mississippi Department of Archives and History, University Press of Mississippi, Mississippi Library Commission, and university personnel and poets in the state to make the selection. We actually select a number of finalists and our state's governor selects the person to become our state's poet laureate for four years. Well, back to the show, we've been talking to Sterling Plumpp and Patrick Oliver. Patrick, I wanted to just continue our conversation from earlier about literacy and impacting the lives of young people, encouraging them, and getting them on board to be critical thinkers and to know something about the world around them by being literate. Are there resources available for the students, to their parents, or to teachers? What can you tell us that you're involved in?

Patrick Oliver: I believe the fact that you mentioned what's available from the Humanities Council, because that was my first grant through the Arkansas Humanities Council. It was a $500 grant. I went to various orga-nizations, saying, "Hey, let me get $500." We brought Tony Medina, who's a poet and writer, to Little Rock, Arkansas, and about nine kids showed up to that writing workshop. We actually published their works, and that became the excitement that came out of Little Rock, Arkansas. It was like, "Wow, you actually published these kids' poetry?" And it was like, "Yes." So I encourage folks to go after mini-grants. Some people say, "Well, it's only $500." Well, you can get $500 here, you can get $500 there, and it adds up and all of a sudden you have enough money to host a very nice public program and buy books for each of the kids that attended. We were able to buy a book for each child that attended. For many of those kids, that was their first autographed book. They've never had a book autographed before. So I encourage folks to do what's necessary to reach out to corporations, to reach out to banks because banks are required through the Community Reinvestment Act to give dollars back to the community. Why not encourage banks to look at literacy because banks need folks in the community to be financially literate. Often times they don't open bank accounts because they've made some mistakes because they weren't financially literate, so they can't open bank accounts. So if you reach out to car dealerships who are in the community, folks are buying cars. So I encourage folks to go to businesses and ask those businesses by creating a one-page letter saying, "Hey, donate $500 to my program. If you don't have $500, give me $200. We'll take that." Do a lot of those letters, but also go after the big dollars as well. Don't be afraid to write a $500,000 proposal. It's an exercise and you may say, "Wow, this is a lot of work." But once you learn how to do that work it becomes beneficial to your organization that you're working with to empower young people. There's a book project that I'm involved with. It was through the Poetry Foundation. It was a publication called *Open the Door: How to Excite Young People about Poetry.* In that publication are lesson plans. We're talking about highly developed youth programs, and they interviewed me about how to raise money for poetry and creative writing programs. So folks, you can get this book for free. It normally costs $20, but today I'm going to tell you how to go on the website (The Poetry Foundation of Chicago) and get the book. It's called *Open the Door: How to Excite Young People about Poetry.* You can go to that website and google the Poetry Foundation and the book title, and the e-book is right there. You can download it. I encourage educators and parents to go out and get it because again it's a very nice book. And the Poetry Foundation is just an incredible organization. They would request like $100,000 from a fiscal member to develop poetry programs for young people all over the country, so this is one of their efforts. They published this book. Even though it's for sale, they have it free to download on their website. And again, there's a section there where I talk about how to raise money for creative writing programs for young people.

Diane Williams: I heard you recently talk at the Margaret Walker Alexander National Research Center about strategies that young people can incorporate into their lives, and as you were talking . . . I'm a mom and I have a genius child by the way who's an engineer and working on his MBA, but anyway the strategies that you mentioned are strategies that I've used with my children and my grandchildren. I think they're utterly important. They're basic things. Tell us a little bit more about those basic strategies that children who just started school not too long ago here in Mississippi can incorporate to fulfill this year and fulfill it successfully.

Patrick Oliver: It's actually what I was talking about. It's actually included in the book that I have coming out. It's called *On My Own: A Vision Board Guidebook for Young People.* And in that I'm just trying to help young people who have asked me for help. All over the country, I get emails. When I go speak at a school, I get emails, just tons of emails from kids saying, "I need help, Mr. Oliver. I need help with this and that." And they're just very basic things that they haven't had a chance to talk to individuals about. So I decided to kind of look at those questions they asked me and compile into some kind of plan for young people. And as adults we, at the beginning of the year, most adults have this plan, this vision board, what we're going to do for the year, New Year's resolutions, and all that. But we never think about the young people. It's so important nowadays for young people to have a strategy for success in their lives. So what I've tried to do is put it in a vision board guidebook to give young people some ideas of what it takes to be successful. I just asked some simple things as, "Have you ever visited a museum or what about a local park?" Going to a local park and just walking every day and enjoying that park that's in your community. "What about the type of food that you eat?" Because we see data now that shows that young people are experiencing high blood pressure at a very young age. I have a chapter that discusses suits for the occasion, just in case you get asked one day to come to do this internship or come to a special ceremony. Are you prepared and do you have a suit? Now, I don't say go buy an expensive suit from Nordstrom. I say, "Hey, go to the local vintage store and see what you can find." When I grew up, you know, we toured the vintage store looking for different clothing. So some basic strategies for life, yeah, are important.

Diane Williams: So this book just came out?
Patrick Oliver: Yep, it just came out.

Diane Williams: And tell us how people could access the book.
Patrick Oliver: They can go to www.speakloudly.com. It's right there on the website. It's entitled *On My Own: A Vison Board Guidebook for Young People.*

Diane Williams: Thank you, thank you very much . . . and Sterling, I haven't forgotten about you. I would like to talk to you a little bit more about the work that you're going to be doing in Mississippi, about poetry. If somebody asked you, "What is poetry?" How would you sum that up? I've got people asking that question.

Sterling Plumpp: I would sum it up the way Gwendolyn Brooks summed it up. Poetry is life, distilled language. Poetry is always a memorable experience.

Diane Williams: And tell me about the poetry you write. What type of poetry? I heard you mention jazz. I heard you mention blues.

Sterling Plumpp: In America or in the university context all literature is defined by the outstanding literary texts that proceed it. So I'm coming after the ode, the sonnet, and the ballad, mastered and made famous by British poets. I'm writing also after three very brilliant and exceptionally well-educated African Americans: Sterling Brown (born 1900 and died 1987, BA from Williams College, MA degree from Harvard) taught Toni Morrison, Ossie Davis, LeRoi Jones, and Stokely Carmichael. He's a brilliant poet who was with Alan Lomax when they originally recorded the likes of Muddy Waters with John W. Work. And so what Sterling Brown did, he made the blues stanza a poetic stanza. Langston Hughes did it in the 1920s. He influenced me heavily, but the poet who had the most direct experience on me was Amiri Baraka who had studied under Sterling Brown at Howard. At the time his name was LeRoi Jones. In the late 1950s and the 1960s, he was a jazz critic for *DownBeat Magazine.* He wrote *Preface to a Twenty Volume Suicide Note,* one of the most important books reflecting on the music and aesthetics of blues people. His poetry is much more free-versed. So when I say I'm a blues poet, I'm looking at cultural antecedents; I'm looking at the way Louis Armstrong or Charlie Parker played. I'm looking at the mood of the metaphor of people ranging from Robert Johnson to B.B. King, to Muddy Waters, to Howlin' Wolf. I'm saying that that music influenced the structure of my poems, as well as the use of metaphor. That's what I'm saying.

Diane Williams: I want to let the listeners know a little bit more about you. Sterling Plumpp has contributed to various anthologies as well as publishing further collections of poetry. He is a poet. He won the Carl Sandburg Literary Prize for Poetry for *The Mojo Hands Call, I Must Go,* and that was in 1983, I believe. He was featured on the Harper Lee Panel for the Mississippi's first statewide book festival, and that was because Harper Lee came out with a new book. I think it was a sequel to *To Kill a Mockingbird*, and so it's the talk of the nation. And so panelists were pulled in almost at the last minute because the book was hot off the press. Then C-SPAN and the Library of Congress came down to get involved in that, so he was considered one of the authorities for discussion of that literature. And he's at Mississippi Valley State University teaching. We have just about a half minute left, so with your final words what would you like to say, Mr. Sterling?

Sterling Plumpp: I would like to say first of all that Mississippi Valley State University is right in the center of American culture and African American culture. Those people who picked the cotton in the Delta produced the most memorable cultural form this country has produced. And the other thing I would like to say, immediately after slavery African Americans turned all of their churches into schools. So Valley and the people of the Delta have a long tradition of establishing a way of educating their young people so that they could make a contribution.

Diane Williams: Final words, Patrick, within five seconds?

Patrick Oliver: Support young people and literacy. Support young people and literacy. Support young people and literacy.

Diane Williams: You have been listening to the *Mississippi Arts Hour* in MPB. I'd like to thank my guests, Sterling Plumpp and Patrick Oliver, for taking time out of their schedules to be here today. If you'd like to listen to this show again or share it with a friend, visit the Arts Commission website (www.arts.ms.gov) where all episodes of the *Arts Hour* are available. The show is available on the MPB website, and be sure to tune in again next weekend for the *Mississippi Arts Hour* on MPB Radio. Thank you for joining us.

(Special thanks to Seprela Ellis of Mississippi Valley State University for her assistance in making this interview transcription possible.)

Bibliography on Sterling D. Plumpp

Articles in Journals, Anthologies, and Books

Allen, Jeffrey Renard. "'Distinguished Breakage': The Jazz Poetry of Sterling D. Plumpp."
Arkansas Review: A Journal of Delta Studies 36.3 (2005): 198–202.

Antonucci, Michael A. "'Crash Down Home Blues': Sterling D. Plumpp, Sterling A. Brown and Blues Poetics." Arkansas Review: A Journal of Delta Studies 36.3 (2005): 205–11.

Cunningham, James. "Baldwinian Aesthetics in Sterling Plumpp's Mojo Poems." Black American Literature Forum 23.3 (1989): 505–18.

———. "Sterling Plumpp." Afro-American Poets since 1955. Dictionary of Literary Biography. Vol. 41. Eds. Trudier Harris and Thadious M. Davis. Detroit: Gale, 1985. 257–65.

Gibbons, Reginald. "Conversations with Sterling D. Plumpp." Arkansas Review: A Journal of Delta Studies 36.3 (2005): 182–93.

Harris, Duriel E. "Epic Voice and the Critical Migrant Body: Approaching Sterling Plumpp's 'Mfua's Song.'" Valley Voices: A Literary Review 9.1 (2009): 13–20.

Jess, Tyehimba. "Sterling Plumpp, Blues Mentor." Valley Voices: A Literary Review 9.1 (2009): 36–43.

———. "A Literary Father's Day." https://aboutaword.wordpress.com/tag/sterling-plumpp/.

Lacava, Jacques. "Sterling Plumpp: A Blues Poet." Living Blues: The Magazine of the African American Blues Tradition 90 (1990): 64–66.

———. "Sterling Plumpp: A Poetry of Chicago Blues" ("Sterling Plumpp: un Poete du Chicago Blues"). Regards Croises sur Chicago. Ed. Sylvie Mathe. Marseille, France: Universite de Provence P, 2004. 227–41. (French).

Lively, Janice Tuck. "Discovering Sterling Plumpp: A Familiar Voice." Valley Voices: A Literary Review 9.1 (2009): 44–51.

McKinney, Maureen Foertsch. "Blues Poet, Chicago Writer Sterling Plumpp Gives the Low-down." Illinois Issues: Art and Ethnicity December 2006. http://illinoisissues-archive.uis.edu/archive/index/index200612.html.

Ndosi, Mankwe. "Magic—A Relationship with the Words of Sterling Plumpp . . . To Be Continued." Valley Voices: A Literary Review 9.1 (2009): 27–31.

Oriol, Marc. "Sterling Plumpp: Mississippi Griot." ABS Magazine (May 2009): 28–33. (French).

Pinson, Hermine. "Telling the Geography of His Horn: Modal Strategies in the Poetry of Sterling Plumpp." *Valley Voices: A Literary Review* 9.1 (2009): 56–78.

Reich, Howard. "Music for the Eyes: Sterling Plumpp Brings the Rush and Rhythms of Jazz to Poetry." *Chicago Tribune* 15 March 1998. sec. 4.

———. "Plumpp's Poetry Embodies the Blues." *Chicago Tribune* 4 June 2013. sec. 4.

Sweeny, Matthew. *The Lottery Wars: Long Odds, Fast Money, and the Battle over an American Institution.* New York: Bloomsbury P, 2009. 61–65.

Ward, Jerry. "Reading Sterling D. Plumpp." http://jerryward.blogspot.com/2013/01/reading -sterling-plumpp.html.

Introductions, Afterword, and Coda

Anania, Michael. "An Introduction to Sterling Plumpp." *Fifth Wednesday Journal* 14 (Spring 2014): 19–21.

Antonucci, Michael A., and Duriel Harris. Coda to the Special Section on Sterling D. Plumpp. *Arkansas Review: A Journal of Delta Studies* 36.3 (2005): 213.

Davis, Thadious M. Foreword to *Home/Bass*. Chicago, Third World P, ix-xii.

Gibbons, Reginald. Introduction to *Home/Bass*. Chicago, Third World P, xiii-xviii.

Harris, Duriel E. "Living Blues: An Introduction to Selected Poems by Sterling Plumpp." *Arkansas Review: A Journal of Delta Studies* 36.3 (2005): 177–78.

Pinson, Hermine, and Duriel E. Harris. Introduction to the Sterling Plumpp Issue. *Valley Voices: A Literary Review* 9.1 (2009): 5–11.

Wideman, John Edgar. Afterword ("Sterling Plumpp's Poetry") to *Blues Narratives*. Chicago: Tia Chucha P, 1999.

Features

Featured in *The Promised Land*, a documentary about the migration of rural Southern blacks from the segregated South to Chicago. 1994.

Featured in *We Are the Blues*. Produced by Anamorphoose Productions for French Television. 1995.

Poetry featured in *Poetry South 2014*.

Poetry featured in *Valley Voices: A Literary Review* 15.2 (2015).

Recorded Poetry/Songs

"Son of the Blues" performed and recorded by Billy Branch and the Chi-Town Hustlers, Red Bean Records. 1984.

"911" performed by Willie Kent and the Gents, Delmar Records. 1993.

"Address in the Streets" performed by Willie Kent and the Gents, Delmar Records. 1996.

"Here I Go, Here I Go" performed by Willie Kent and the Gents, Blue Chicago Records. 2002.

Poetry reading in celebrating the National Poetry Month at MVSU, accompanied by jazz
saxophonist Alphonso Sanders and percussionist Ben Arnold. April 2015.

Book Reviews

Allen, Kimberly. Rev. of *Home/Bass*. *Valley Voices: A Literary Review* 13.2 (2013): 116–18.

Antonucci, Michael A. Rev. of *Velvet BeBop Kente Cloth*. *African American Review* 39.1–2
(2005): 257–59.

Bonair-Agard, Roger. Rev. of *Velvet BeBop Kente Cloth*. *Black Issues Book Review* 5.2 (2003): 30.

Burns, Ann, and Barbara Hoffert. Rev. of *Ornate with Smoke*. *Library Journal* 18 (128): 107.

Davenport, Doris. "Black American Poetry in the Eighties: Book Reviews" (Rev. of *The Mojo
Hands Call, I Must Go*). *Black American Literature Forum* 17.4 (Autumn 1983): 177–79.

Dulcy, Brainard, and Sybil S. Steinberg. Rev. of *Ornate with Smoke*. *Publishers Weekly* 244.26
(1997): 74.

Fontenot, Chester J. Rev. of *Clinton*. *Black American Literature Forum* 11.3 (Autumn 1977): 119.

Gilyard, Keith. Rev. of *Ornate with Smoke*. *African American Review* 34.1 (2000): 178–80.

Jess, Tyehimba. Rev. of *Blues Narratives*. *Black Issues Book Review* 3.1 (2001): 30–31.

Lurie, Carol. Rev. of *Somehow We Survive*. *Library Journal* 107.7 (1982): 731.

Moore, Lenard D. Rev. of *Blues: The Story Always Untold*. *Library Journal* 114.11 (1989): 61.

Ratner, Rochelle. Rev. of *The Mojo Hands Call, I Must Go*. *Library Journal* 107.22 (1982): 2342.

Rochman, Hazel. Rev. of *Johannesburg & Other Poems*. *Booklist* 90.1 (1993): 28.

Thompson, Mark. Rev. of *Home/Bass*. *Blues Blast Magazine* 7–35 (August 29, 2013). http://
www.thebluesblast.com/Archive/BluesBlasts/2013/BluesBlast8_29_13.htm

Wright, John. Rev. of *Horn Man*. *Chicago Review* 41.2–3 (1995): 164–67.

Index

96, 100, 108, 111, 113, 117, 123–24,
126, 132, 145–46, 149, 155, 163; on
black men and women, 39, 62, 70;
on blackness, 25, 33, 45–46, 65,
68, 74, 76, 113; on blues and jazz,
5–6, 49, 53, 78, 110, 123–24, 154; on
brother, 14, 33, 59, 78; on church,
4, 6, 18, 22, 24, 29, 31, 43–46, 58,
97, 110, 113–15, 133, 144–45, 147,
150–51, 154, 169; on critics and
scholars, 25, 52, 71, 111; on decolonization, 48; on democracy, 29;
on education, 8, 25, 40, 44, 47–48,
53, 60, 78, 93, 113–14, 155, 162–63;
on father, 14, 18, 22, 29, 37, 69, 112,
161; on forms, meter, and rhythm,
22, 31–34, 53–54, 56, 65, 76, 87, 97,
99–100, 110–11, 117–18, 123–24,
126–27, 133–35, 143, 147, 154; on
genre, 100, 110, 114, 142, 153, 156;
on God, religion, and prayer, 8, 19,
37, 43–44, 54, 58, 61, 66, 82, 110,
113, 119, 121, 123–24, 132, 154; on
Gospel music, 17–18, 21, 32, 34,
44–45, 110, 122, 124, 141, 145, 159;
on grandfather, 14–15, 18, 32, 37,
50, 57–60, 67, 80, 85–86, 113, 115,
120, 150, 154, 159, 161; on grandmother, 14, 32, 37, 57–59, 86, 150,
154, 162; on history and ancestors,
12, 16, 31, 37, 51–52, 55, 65–66,
68–69, 71–72, 78–79, 85–86, 97,
99, 109, 112, 115, 120, 122–23, 128,
141, 156, 158–59; on identity, 27,
66, 71, 139; on imagination, 40,
52–54, 60–61, 68–69, 74, 77–78,
82, 85–86, 89–90, 93, 117, 123, 125,
131, 133, 136, 143, 154; on improvisation, 11, 52–53, 79, 84, 100, 117,
124, 156; on influences, 3, 20, 44,

74, 81, 96, 99, 110, 113–14, 118, 120,
125–26, 140, 146, 148, 155, 168;
on mother, 14–16, 18–19, 37, 43,
53, 56, 58–59, 85, 95, 112, 115, 120,
156, 162; on music, 3, 7, 18–20,
31–32, 37, 44–45, 49, 52–56, 63,
78–79, 81–85, 90–91, 93, 96, 98,
110–11, 116, 118, 120, 123–28,
131–33, 135–36, 139–40, 143–50,
153–54, 168; on his name, 161–62;
on race, 29, 39, 71, 114; on racism,
69, 92, 128; on slavery, 13, 43, 51,
59–60, 67–68, 71, 83, 159, 169; on
South Africa, 8, 20, 28, 36, 38–39,
41, 48–50, 66, 78–79, 86, 92, 94,
98–99, 129, 131, 152; on style, 25,
97–99, 118, 121, 135–36, 142; on
trans-Atlantic slave trade, 48

Works: "Address in the Street," 133,
172; "Autobiographical Essay,"
12–13, 23, 34; *Black Rituals*, xix,
25, 32, 38, 43, 46–47, 110, 113, 115;
Blues Narratives, xi, xiv, xxi, 43,
50, 52–53, 60, 67, 85, 88–89, 95,
101, 105, 107, 112–13, 115, 120, 153,
171; *Blues: The Story Always Untold*, xx, 11, 35–36, 39, 66, 86, 91,
94, 98, 132, 153, 172; "Blues/scapes,"
11; *Clinton*, xix, 21, 25, 32–33, 35,
38, 66, 91, 113, 172; "Eight," 119;
"Fractured Dreams," xix, 21, 35;
"From the Delta," 133; *From South
Africa*, 39; "Gathering Place," 138;
Half Black Half Blacker, xviii, 25,
31–33, 38, 45, 66, 94, 158; "Healing
Music," 116; *Home/Bass*, ix, xi, xvi,
xxii, 113, 117, 120, 122, 124, 130–41,
148–50, 153–54, 171–72; *Horn
Man*, xi, xx, 66–67, 82, 84, 88–89,
94, 98, 153, 158, 172; "I Hear the